SELLING IN THE QUALITY ERA

D1621893

This book is dedicated to all those businesspersons
who pursue their natural self-interest by providing
legitimate and beneficial products and services
to their fellow man.

SELLING IN THE QUALITY ERA

George H. Peeler

BLACKWELL
Business

Copyright © Peeler, George H., 1996

The right of George H. Peeler, to be identified as author of this work has been
asserted in acordance with the Copyright, Designs and Patents Act 1988.

First published 1996

Blackwell Publishers Inc.
238 Main Street
Cambridge, Massachusetts 02142
USA

Blackwell Publishers Ltd.
108 Cowley Road
Oxford OX4 1JF
UK

Library of Congress Cataloging-in-Publication Data
Peeler, George, 1942–
    Selling in the quality era / George Peeler.
        p.   cm.
    ISBN 1-55786-666-X (pb)
    1. Selling—Quality control.   2. Sales management.   I. Title.
HF5438.25.P43 1996
658.8'1—dc20   95-31594
                                                                        CIP

British Library Cataloguing in Publication Data

A CIP catalogue record for this book is available from the British Library.

Typset by Cornerstone Composition Services.

Printed in the USA on acid-free paper.

CONTENTS

Contents

3 Personal Professional Selling in the Quality Era 58

4 The Sales Personality 77

5 The Buying Decision 91

6 The Sales Continuum 117

Contents

Contents

List of Figures

ACKNOWLEDGMENTS

This work has grown out of the combined efforts and observations of many people. I owe a great debt to the IBM Company and its sales people, too numerous to mention, whose studied excellence in the art of selling has lent so much to me across my career and produced many of the thoughts presented.

I appreciate the encouragement of the staff of the College of Business at the University of Tennessee and their many positive suggestions. Individuals whose help is particularly appreciated include Harlan Caruthers, William Cole, Hans Jensen, and series editor Michael Stahl, who felt strongly that a book written from the salesperson's and salesmanager's perspective and based on practical experience would add positively to the literature being now produced relating to the quality movement.

I wish also to thank Daniel Shore, Product Marketing Manager, ēlo TouchSystems, for his critique and suggestions and A. B. Coleman, president of Quality Development, Inc., for his advice. I appreciate the efforts of my typist, Ms. Nancy Arflack. My thanks also to my wife, Molly, who encouraged me to assemble notes taken over the years from my reading and experience and to incorporate them into a book.

Last, but certainly not least, I wish to thank the many writers of earlier times who continually reminded us that we must consider the human side of economics or all our business strategies gain us nothing. The Quality Era is reaffirming this truth.

ABOUT THE AUTHOR

George Peeler has been a salesman and a student of selling since childhood, when he sold lemonade, vegetables, and greeting cards. After gaining a degree in zoology and animal behavior from the University of Tennessee in 1964, he joined Wyeth Laboratories as a pharmaceutical sales representative. Five years later, he joined IBM as a territory sales representative in Memphis, Tennessee, and within four years was named IBM's top national new account computer salesman. He went on to assist with the design and implementation of a new IBM sales training program in Atlanta, Georgia, and served on the staff of this facility for two years, after which he was promoted to marketing manager in Tulsa, Oklahoma. A series of promotions followed: to marketing programs in Atlanta, to senior marketing representative in Memphis, and then to senior academic specialist with statewide marketing responsiblity for IBM sales to all higher educational institutions in Tennessee. During his 22-year career with IBM, Mr. Peeler gave numerous lectures on sales in the United States, Canada, and Europe. He left IBM in 1992.

Mr. Peeler has gained a broad range of experience from IBM and from owning his own business, a retail mens clothing store. Mr. Peeler makes his home in Knoxville, Tennessee. He and his wife, Molly, a Knoxville physician, have four children. Today, Mr. Peeler does independent sales consulting and serves as board member and marketing advisor to several Knoxville area technology development firms.

INTRODUCTION

Business success in the new global economy will depend on the ability to establish differentiating product value through quality in design and production – and in communicating that value effectively to the customer. In the worldwide marketplace there will almost always be others who can price lower. Competing strictly in the commodity or price arenas can mean lower profits, ever-increasing competition, and business decline. A superior strategy, therefore, is to sell to and retain customers through value based on quality. Increasing levels of quality are becoming the norm even for commodity products. The fact that *perceived product quality* is emerging as the most important competitive factor in modern business leads to our labelling the current business epoch the "Quality Era."

Within most businesses, the task of personalizing and communicating product value through interactive discussion is the task of a personal sales group. It is to the executive management, the marketing and sales managers, the sales trainers, and the sales personnel of these companies that this book is directed. Sales and marketing students will also find in this book realistic insights into the challenges of modern selling.

In the Quality Era, a broader view of personal selling that emphasizes quality must be achieved. Innovative integration of the sales group within the business organization must also be accomplished to complement quality initiatives in product design and production. This will greatly facilitate the communication of quality-based value to customers.

Much recent attention has been given to the application of total quality principles to the design and production segments of business, often with positive results. Little, if any, emphasis, however, has been given to "quality" in selling and the sales process. There are several reasons for this.

Design and production naturally involve precise, objective

1

standards that offer visible opportunities for the institution and measurement of quality-oriented procedures. The applicability of total quality concepts to more abstract areas such as marketing and personal selling can be less obvious. Executive management can also believe that there is ample work ahead implementing quality programs in production alone. Sales management may consider that their group already deals intimately with customer attitudes and thus already comprehends this ultimate focus of quality initiatives. As a further complicating factor, there has been little if any literature linking quality concepts to professional selling.

This must change. Both modern and historical quality concepts can be directly applied to the challenges of Quality Era selling. Global competition is requiring a new focus for professional salespeople, both in customer situations and within the vendor organization. An older, restricted vision of personal selling must give way to new process concepts that more effectively communicate the quality of the product to the customer. Even earlier in the cycle, business organizations must provide effective assistance in designing products that will sell. If quality is not perceived and appreciated by customers, the quality attained in production is in vain.

The suggestions and concepts presented in this book should not prove unduly difficult to implement. They are based on both experience and observation and can have a profound impact on overall business performance.

Field sales personnel will find here perspectives and techniques to help ensure that their sales efforts meet the unique challenges of selling value based on quality completely and effectively. Sales and marketing managers will encounter structured concepts for developing a more effective and productive sales team. Business managers at all levels may gain deeper insight into the mentality and attitudes of their salespeople and thus discover enhanced possibilities for using the sales force to communicate crucially important customer attitudes and reactions within the organization. Marketing or sales students should come to understand more clearly the realities of personal selling and the new challenges of Quality Era professional selling.

I once commented to one of my consulting customer managers that a single good idea could be worth a million dollars, to which he replied, "I agree. Which one is it?" It was a good question. One cannot predict which specific concepts will best fit a particular business or salesperson. I do believe that the principles mentioned herein can, if understood and implemented, have substantive positive effect. If some appear simplistic, it is because they represent a distillation of concept. Many valuable concepts owe their usefulness to the fact that they can be stated simply and understood easily. Their truth is often intuitively obvious.

Modern quality principles have perhaps been best summarized by the late Dr. W. Edwards Deming, whose 14 points of quality are frequently used as validation of the concepts presented in this book. As we shall see, there are other sources from which supplemental perspectives to build a new foundation for selling in the Quality Era can be drawn. The role of perspective cannot be overemphasized. Perspective governs both our approach and our actions. A proper perspective is essential, for as Dr. Deming expressed, pursuing quality does not just call for doing the obvious with more vigor.[1] The effective implementation of quality innovations requires a new and broadened philosophy. Selling must be seen from a system and process viewpoint and therefore be subject to measurement and continuous improvement. Indeed, the entire vendor business should move toward becoming a *selling organization*.

In the first chapter, an historical perspective of key market principles is presented. These concepts are the underpinnings of the modern marketplace, which has brought about an unprecedented and very recent revolution in the quality of human life. Market mechanisms discussed years ago foreshadow modern discussions of quality concepts in products and in selling.

Chapter 2 is a look at the challenges and causes of market changes that are part of the new sales arena, the global marketplace.

Today's professional salesperson must address heightened competition and customer expectations. Quality Era salespeople must participate more effectively *inside their companies* to

3

assist in developing products that will sell. Chapter 3 gives new perspectives on both the internal and external roles for sales organizations.

The interpersonal skills of an individual can determine his or her effectiveness in professional selling. Selling is, in fact, part art and part science. Because effective salespeople tend to identify strongly with their customers, they can appear detached from the central business organization. Business executives frequently have had little or no sales experience. In the Quality Era, these two groups need to understand one another more fully. Chapter 4 offers insights into the common aspects of a sales personality, for if the sales group is to be integrated more effectively into the business, it must be understood and appreciated by upper management.

"The Buying Decision," presented in Chapter 5, is a Quality Era structured sales process that looks at value from the customer's point of view and is designed to ensure a more complete selling process that produces more knowledgeable and committed customers. These customers will then come to view the vendor organization as a dependable supplier of product. A methodology is offered for determining whether or not components of a sales construction are missing, which can cause customer doubt, lack of commitment, and lost sales.

Quality Era personal selling should be perceived as a process – a sales continuum. When viewed from this perspective and monitored effectively, continuous quality improvement becomes possible and the business moves toward becoming a *selling organization*. This concept is developed in Chapter 6.

Chapter 7 examines how selling and the sales support process can be measured and given structure by a quality methodology. Selling is, to a degree, an art, but it is an art amenable to systematization, measurement, and improvement.

Chapter 8 suggests how this methodology can lead to the development of products that are consistent with the *customer's* concept of value. These products can then be sold with enthusiasm by the sales force and produced with commitment by the design and production teams. The business can become infused with enthusiasm and pride.

The development of a Quality Era selling business will require leadership from management in engaging and motivating employees. Chapter 9 suggests mechanisms by which a unifying vision, shared by both management and employees, can be achieved to the betterment of the business.

Throughout the text, the reader will encounter a number of references and examples drawn from the author's experiences within the IBM Corporation. IBM has recently encountered difficulties, mostly due to a dramatic explosion of available computer power at rapidly deteriorating prices. The instances related are included simply as examples that are common to modern business. In many ways, IBM focused on quality before quality was a defined concept. There is, I believe, no business in the world where one could have gained more useful experience in selling and in management, but even IBM has not been immune to the need for change.

The concepts and methodologies presented herein are the result of many years of varied experience in selling, sales management, sales consulting and business ownership—experience that has ranged from computers to prescription pharmaceuticals. They arise from actual experience in what works and what does not. They are based on a belief that a sound, empathetic philosophy of business must be added to the increasingly dry and mechanistic marketing methodologies that imply that customers can be dealt with from a detached perspective. Such a synergy of the subjective and the objective aspects of business is needed to form a more correct Quality Era selling perspective from which will flow the products, strategies, processes, and, ultimately, the atmosphere that can make a modern business great.

References

[1]   Neave, H. R., 1990. *The Deming Dimension.* Knoxville, TN: SPC Press, p. 30

CHAPTER 1

HISTORICAL PERSPECTIVE

The Quality Era

The Quality Era began in July 1950 when an American expert in manufacturing efficiency and statistical quality control began briefings with the leaders of Japanese industry. The American was Dr. W. Edwards Deming, and the briefings led to a commitment on the part of the largest and most influential Japanese firms to adopt statistical quality control techniques as a central focus for manufacturing.[1] These procedures had been developed earlier in the United States; they had been studied academically but had found only limited application in industry. In Japan, these procedures were adopted and followed with almost total commitment. The results were dramatic. Within a few years, Japan moved from a national image of cheap shoddiness in its manufactured goods to a position of worldwide respect for its product quality. The wealth and status that accompanied this achievement propelled Japan rapidly from relative insignificance into the first tier of the world's industrialized nations.

The introduction and adoption of a powerful innovative business concept thus created a new competitive era, one in which new standards for product quality and value were established. The quality of products made in Japan began to set product performance and value standards for manufacturers in other nations. Quality had, of course, always been an incidental objective for most manufactured products, but the new Japanese offerings in optics, electronics, and automobiles were the direct result of their direct emphasis on – and commitment to – specific, scientific principles of quality production. These methods led to products of innovative design and outstanding performance that were sold at prices below those of similar products offered by other nations. A new, competitive value dimension had been introduced that required other nations and their industries to either catch up or drop out. National reputations for superior manufacturing quality shifted, demonstrating that a superior concept, implemented with commitment, can result in new dimensions of business performance. Customers and those who wished to make and sell products came to expect new levels of product quality sold at more competitive prices.

Deming's statistical production quality methods were paralleled by a philosophical approach to business that enabled the quality methodology. Deming had emphasized that, unless this broader, *quality philosophy* was adopted simultaneously with new production techniques, quality results could not be achieved. The statistical measurement and management of production quality were themselves an outgrowth of a philosophy that emphasized looking without preconceptions at how businesses were operated. Only with an open mind that could study objectively and scientifically what was actually occurring could the reality of business situations be comprehended and productive innovation accomplished. The power behind the physical changes that result from such knowledge is a philosophical approach to business operation out of which flows quality products, customer delight, worker satisfaction, pride in accomplishment, growth, and business success.

These concepts also suggest that personal monetary gain for business management and owners should be pursued obliquely and not as the prime agenda. If management's focus is constantly on short-term earnings, attention will not be on the factors that actually lead to sustained profit and business longevity.

Several earlier writers suggested similar subjective principles, often with remarkable foresight. Their ideas were at times brushed aside in the rush toward producing and selling in the growth economies of the last two centuries; their worth was not then apparent to business. In the Quality Era, we must listen. Success in this new age must be earned by offering the customer unprecedented levels of quality and value. The emerging quality philosophy that is now revolutionizing manufacturing and design must be echoed in other areas of business, including marketing and the selling process. Product quality is an essential component of value, and value perception is the focus and motive force in selling.

Deming corroborated the work done by these great historical visionaries on quality and value. He actually demonstrated in the arena of international business the superiority of quality-oriented methods and philosophy. Deming presented new statistical quality methods and a new philosophy of business to the Japanese, whose resultant product quality "changed the economy of the world." The differentiating issue in the global market – product value through quality – is now settled. Businesses that wish to compete successfully must now do so on a basis of quality.

A Review of the Deming Philosophy

Many texts have been written that deal exclusively with Deming's philosophy and principles, but an overview can be presented here. These principles were being refined and expanded right up until his death. The precepts outlined here sum up the essentials.

Deming summarized his message as "management for quality." He emphasized that "a quality philosophy must pervade the business organization and this can only be instituted and communicated from committed top management. The paramount focus of a business organization must be to delight the customer. Customers are delighted when they get more usefulness in a product than they expected. The effort to do even better for the customer must be continuous and unrelenting". Deming stressed that many of the most crucial factors concerning business performance are not amenable to numerical quantification and must be approached subjectively; in fact, it is most important to understand the limitations of purely numerical techniques: "The most important figures needed for management of any organization are often unknown and indeed unknowable."[2] Deming frequently restated this quote by Dr. Lloyd Nelson, Director of statistical methods, Nasua Corporation.

The business must come to function as a team with the

long-range and immediate focus of fulfilling the unrelenting objective of *customer delight* through the delivery of excellence in product quality and value. These objectives are to be achieved through the consistent implementation of quality-focused management philosophy and business principles.

Mere lip service to these objectives will not meet the new demands of the global market. The correcting of mistakes and errors in products must be replaced by business approaches that do not produce mistakes and errors in the first place. If the input components are quality and the process is quality, the final result will reliably be quality. In this regard, suppliers of materials and components should not be selected solely on price but also on the ability to deliver in a timely fashion the best components as required in order to achieve the consistent quality in production mentioned previously. The inspection of the final product must be de-emphasized; the way to ensure quality is to perfect the production process.

Management must facilitate the processes of quality innovation through prompt action, removing barriers to employee performance by continually attending to *process* improvement. These actions should accompany a movement from management bossism to *leadership in innovation and facilitation* made in concert with employees. Management openness, accessibility, and leadership eliminate employee fear and reticence, which will then allow employee creativity and enthusiasm to flow toward their work and their company. Pride in work ensues; joy in work follows. The team spirit of the business must be such that interdepartmental barriers and rivalry are eliminated so that employees mix easily and communicate openly about achieving the business's overall quality objectives. Exhortations to work harder are replaced by pride in work and the company. Employees are encouraged toward self-improvement through company support for education and other measures toward self-actualization. The business demonstrates genuine care and concern for the personal development of its workers, who respond with loyalty. Arbitrary numerical measurements of individual and departmental performance through quotas are eliminated.

Deming felt that the limitations of the systems and processes within which employees are required to work have much more effect on their achievements than their own efforts. For him, business has only one essential measurement: customer delight, a team measurement that applies to the entire enterprise. Only the highest levels of company management have the authority to make the systemwide changes necessary to successfully implement quality methods and philosophy.

As contemporary American business operations, including selling, are reviewed against these points, it can be seen that in many cases they are diametrically opposed to Deming's concepts. There are, of course, many ways to run a business, and other methodologies and philosophies have met with measures of success – in the past. They may not be sufficient in the Quality Era.

Deming challenged the status quo with a new philosophy. That philosophy is now proving its superiority through results. An effective philosophy is the most powerful of mental armaments, for out of philosophy arises perspective. When perspective is accurate, strategy and performance can be brought to bear with great result. When philosophy is in error, energies are dissipated fighting reality. The challenge is to identify philosophical truth that may be applied to business, selling, and to life in general. Success, then, ensues for us and for those we serve.

Deming's 14 Points

Deming's philosophy is based on 14 points that can be applied anywhere – to small organizations as well as to large ones, to the service industry as well as to manufacturing.[3] They apply to a division within a company. They apply to a product development group. As we shall see, they apply to sales organizations. These 14 points are to:

1. Create constancy of purpose toward improvement of product and service with the aim to become competitive and to stay in business, and to provide jobs.
2. Adopt the new philosophy. We are in a new economic age. Western management must awaken to the chal-

lenge, must learn their responsibilities, and take on leadership for change.
3. Cease dependence on inspection to achieve quality. Eliminate the need for inspection on a mass basis by building quality into the product in the first place.
4. End the practice of awarding business on the basis of price tag. Instead, minimize total cost. Move toward a single supplier for any one item, on a long-term relationship of loyalty and trust.
5. Improve constantly and forever the system of production and service, to improve quality and productivity, and thus constantly decrease costs.
6. Institute training on the job.
7. Institute leadership. The aim of supervision should be to help people and machines and gadgets to do a better job. Supervision of management is in need of overhaul, as well as supervision of production workers.
8. Drive out fear, so that everyone may work effectively for the company.
9. Break down barriers between departments. People in research, design, sales, and production must work as a team, to foresee problems first of production and in use that may be encountered with the product or service.
10. Eliminate slogans, exhortations, and targets for the work force asking for zero defects and new levels of productivity. Such exhortations only create adversarial relationships, as the bulk of the causes of low quality and low productivity belong to the system and thus lie beyond the power of the work force.
11a. Eliminate work standards (quotas) on the factory floor. Substitute leadership.
11b. Eliminate management by objective. Eliminate management by numbers, numerical goals. Substitute leadership.
12a. Remove barriers that rob the hourly worker of his right to pride of workmanship. The responsibility of supervisors must be changed from sheer numbers to quality.
12b. Remove barriers that rob people in management and in

engineering of their right to pride of workmanship. This means, inter alia, the abolishment of the annual or merit rating and of management by objective.

13. Institute a vigorous program of education and self-improvement.
14. Put everybody in the company to work to accomplish the transformation. The transformation is everybody's job.

Deming's quality philosophy, as demonstrated in these points, has many facets. As much as anything, they register a call away from purely objective functional "management" toward inclusion of subjective reality to produce "leadership." Deming is yet another historic voice reminding society and business that subjective realities are of essential importance. Selling is and has always been subjective activity at the interpersonal level. Deming himself said that one-third of the good results flow from statistical quality methods and the other two-thirds come from how we treat people.[1]

Historical Quality Concepts

Patterns scarcely discernible in the past often emerge full-grown in the future. The modern global marketplace is such a manifestation. Its roots are deep in history. It has been emerging for centuries. Its present status is only the latest – and possibly not the last – major stage of economic change.

A brief review of history reveals that major economic changes have occurred whenever a confluence of discovery, invention, or facilitation permits. These produce major breaks with the past that define the resultant new era. Recent mechanization, followed by improved communications and transportation advances, have enabled the expansions of markets to their new global scale.

The modern global market and the Quality Era have arrived simultaneously. Business faces a new situation; the concepts that allowed success in the old may be inappropriate in the new. In times of great change, it can be reassuring to identify those things that have not changed. These constants can thus provide anchor points in a sea of change. From these vantage points, the new economic era can be seen as a natural outgrowth, an expected evolutionary step capable of benefiting those who understand and seize its opportunities. It will devastate many who do not.

It has been observed that people might be divided into three groups: those who make things happen, those who watch things happen, and those who ask, "What happened?" The successful business of today must make things happen. The change in the marketplace necessitates a change in strategy. Those who wait too late to change may ask "What happened?" from a much weakened economic position. Sales and selling must also change.

The Marketplace – The Arena of Trade

Humans have engaged in trade since prehistoric times. The earliest writings give clear evidence of commerce. Discoveries of stone objects and pottery in locations far from their origins indicate widespread exchange of items among even the most ancient cultures. One can surmise that ever since things have been grown or fashioned there have been both excesses and deficiencies of goods and differences in their quality as well. The desire to acquire the useful and to obtain it in exchange for the less useful has produced the market, situations or places of exchange, of buying and selling.

The trade of earliest times was chiefly barter for agricultural products, and quantities of agricultural commodities were used to measure wealth and value. Homer's Iliad relates that one Greek warrior's armor was priced in terms of so many black cattle.[4] Similarly, in verse 1:3 of Job, one of the oldest books in the Bible, Job's wealth is measured in terms of sheep, camels, and oxen. Agricultural development and domestication of live-stock made food sources dependable, allowing the stabilization of communities where mankind could build towns for protection and engage in centralized trade.

Such agricultural commodity-based wealth is perishable. Only a limited amount of the possessions of a wealthy individual could be used directly in the maintenance of the owner and his immediate family; the remainder was used in securing and retaining followers to help as servants and soldiers. The major motivation was maintaining life and health. The human race may well have been much more indolent than today; the motivation of consumerism had not arrived. The average person had little with which to trade. Scant variety was visible or available.

Since wealth was generally consumable, clan size and military strength were the status measurements of the day. Precious stones and metals were kept and traded at times by the highest orders of society, but were generally too rare for the common people to possess and use in common exchange. The invention of coined money is quite ancient. It offered many advantages to early people, including portability, permanence, and a medium of exchange, but the material choices of life were severely limited until several hundred years ago. There were great works of art, architecture, and literature, but these were most often one-of-a-kind or custom items subsidized by patrons and available only to the highest levels of society.

The average person's material choices were much more bland. His or her options were limited to merchandise such as butcher's beef and baker's bread – commodity-level items with little differentiation. Nevertheless, history paints a picture of the village market as a stimulating social gathering place – pigs, chickens, and all. The earliest selling was quite possibly vendors crying out in the market to attract the attention of passersby to their goods, or a merchant rolling out his wares before a nobleman.[5]

A market or a specific place of trade was a feature of all towns and cities. It is interesting to consider whether the formation of villages and, ultimately, cities was due as much to a desire for safety and protection as for the facilitation of centralized trade. Regardless, as the wealth of cities grew through trade, the need for protection of that wealth increased, necessitating defensive structures and military organizations. Legal structures for governing procedures in the market and protecting wealth became necessary as cities concentrated wealth that became more portable and as greater disparities developed between levels of society. Trade and selling, to a great degree, have thus driven the development of civilization—its structures, its laws, and its organizations.

The Driving Force – A Desire for Betterment

Until recent times, each human was thought to be born to his or her fixed niche in the social order. This social positioning was ordained by a divine power. The individual was to keep his or her divinely decreed place in the social and religious orders throughout his or her lifetime. The idea of a segment of life called "economic" had not yet fully dawned.[6] The belief that any but the nobility and clergy should possess and exhibit material wealth was an alien concept. Opulence might have been dreamed about, but privately. How to achieve it was not clear within the confines of the religious and social structure. Education that could stimulate the imagination was also limited. To harbor ambition, much less to stir it up through *selling*, was a sin. In fact man's original sinful act, followed by disastrous consequences, was attributed to ambition for things not divinely ordained. Satan, pictured in the form of a dishonest salesperson, suggested to Eve that the forbidden fruit was good for food and pleasing to the eye and could make one wise. Satan's appeal was thus to lust of the flesh, of the eye and of the pride of life. Three value perspectives very much alive today. [Genesis 3:6] Man was to keep his place and be thankful for what God had given him. This was the accepted thought pattern for thousands of years.[7]

By about the middle of the 14th century, the stimulation of exploration and discovery was increasing trade in Europe. The resulting economic growth produced more requirements for craftspeople to build and make items for trade. People began to be paid in wages. The great feudal domains were broken up. Serfs became "free" laborers, which led to increases in production as well as an improved standard of living. A greater variety of products became more accessible. When this factor was combined with the growing numbers of wage-earning customers, a dramatic growth in markets resulted. Improvements in the financial status of larger segments of the population opened the way for education, political power, and entrepreneurship. A broadening of education encouraged developments in literature and the arts and sciences, and the growing middle class, now educated, began to react to the instinctive human urge to improve one's lot through the acquisition of things to increase one's comfort.

The open market stalls of earlier times evolved into stores and shops offering permanence, security, and increasing variety. These became business "establishments." Reputations for quality and value had always been associated with certain shops and craftspeople, but as their numbers increased, so did the differentiation between them. Vendors coveted endorsement and trade with noted persons of the day as avidly as today's businesses seek the endorsement of celebrities and sports figures. Even today shops in England display the coat of arms of the royal family, indicating that the vendor is a "provisioner to Royalty."

Selling effort was often confined simply to the reputation of the business and a business sign above the door. In open markets, however, vendors called to passersby to "come, look, and buy," as they do today in the open city markets of the world. Until the 16th century, most of the wholesale buying and selling in Europe was conducted in open trade fairs. Economies now began rapid growth as a result of stimulus from travel, education, exploration, and military expeditions, all of which enlightened more and more of the populace and opened new vistas for creative enterprise.

Around 1600, a major expansion of the European economy took place. This was the result of many converging factors. Trade was producing wealth for the emerging middle class in unprecedented proportions. This class, now having some capital to invest in further economic endeavors and in acquiring more opulent accouterments of life, stimulated further expansion of the economies of Europe. The growth in middle-class wealth also provided larger numbers of people with political power, and they began to question the total control of the ruling class.[8] Concepts of social mobility and of individual rights began to take shape, and laws and governments moved to accommodate these new directions. Broader education of greater numbers of people injected more creativity into society.

Early industry was cottage bound. People who were basically farmers produced in their homes products for sale in the market to supplement their livelihood. Manufacturing was only incidental to agriculture. Limitations of the agricultural technology of the day required that the majority of the population be dedicated to farming. These were restraints, but with colonial trade and gradual improvements in agriculture and manufacturing technology, the standard of living for the average person improved. The increase in trade led to a need for financial innovation, and banking and finance developed as institutions and areas of expertise in support of this expansion.

Gradually, the increasing availability of items that enhanced the comfort and convenience of human life, combined with specialized trades that were making earnings available with which to buy goods, began to rouse humanity from its indolence into industry and creativity. To the religious and social orders of existence, an economic side was being added. The focus on the basics of food, clothing, and shelter that throughout history had occupied almost all available time came to be directed toward business and enterprise, which offered new ways to make life better. Human existence was moving from dependence on self-production or hierarchical provision to dependence on success in the marketplace.

Selling as a Dishonorable Vocation

From earliest history, merchants or those salespeople who traded goods for gain were viewed as odious and despicable characters. The *Odyssey* records Ulysses as affronted by being asked whether he was a pirate or a merchant. (The two were considered about equal.) As he was a military man with a reputation for bravery, he was reckoned a pirate and therefore treated with some honor. To perform a service or give anything without a reward was thought to be generous and noble, but to barter one thing for another was considered mean or low.[9]

Up through the 18th century, the trade of a merchant was

deprecated and considered contemptible in Europe. This attitude often confined merchants to the lowest ranks of society. It was difficult for these individuals to raise necessary capital. Licenses, fees, and taxes placed upon them were onerous. All these barriers severely hampered the progress of commerce. Even laws requiring customer payment to merchants were lax. Yet, in spite of all these barriers, trade grew dramatically and living standards were improved by it. The desire for betterment through trade was stronger than its resistant forces.

As the opportunities offered by increasing knowledge, the availability of products, and the means for acquiring them became more visible, motivation increased. Personal motivation fed creativity and innovation in the production processes, which in turn led to specialization of labor functions by workers and a further boost in productivity and income.

When in the late 1700s industry began to move into factory settings with mechanized production, output and efficiency took a dramatic leap forward. The application of scientific knowledge began to replace stagnating superstition. Technology was used to harness the powers of nature to produce, through machines, exponentially more goods at exponentially faster rates. This made unprecedented comforts available to all levels of society at increasingly lower prices.

The world was ready for the goods that were produced. The Industrial Revolution was a turning point in human history, and it began only two centuries ago. It continues today, accelerated by technological improvements on all fronts and two new components – unprecedented communication coupled with rapid transportation. The Industrial Revolution is the foundation of the new global market and the Quality Era.

Adam Smith

In 1776, a Scottish professor of moral philosophy published a world-changing work entitled *The Wealth of Nations*.[2] With remarkable insight, Adam Smith outlined the key principles at work in the growing economic engine of Europe and explained its internal forces. Smith observed that the division and specialization of labor allowed increased production efficiencies and, therefore, increases in wealth. Not only individual gain but the very wealth and well-being of each nation depended on its efficiency of production and trade, which in turn depended on human motivation.

Smith observed that an innate self-interest on the part of each human being to seek his or her own betterment provides the essential fuel for the whole economic process. The market regulates itself in terms of supply and demand, which interact to establish price. The price of anything can be related to demand and to the amount of skill, risk, and labor necessary to produce or acquire it. Different types of labor are priced at different levels, and this, too, is regulated by supply and demand.

Smith's writing was extraordinarily timely, for the governments of Europe were not at all in agreement as to what role government should play in their newly erupting economies. Smith demonstrated the benefits of limited government intervention and advocated free trade where possible. He pointed out ways in which government might facilitate the process of production and trade to better a nation and its people. Smith had the unique vision to present a comprehensive model of the functioning of national economies and of the essential principles underlining their operation. His purpose was to provide a perspective for governments to use in formulating legislation to assist economic growth and to point out the destructive nature of restrictive law. *The Wealth of Nations* was widely read and acclaimed in Smith's own time, and his recommendations concerning laws and economy (the study of which came to be called "political economics") were accepted and implemented broadly across Europe, unleashing trade and production from the legal and social barriers that had worked against them until that time.

Smith is recognized today as the founder of modern economics, and *The Wealth of Nations* still ranks as one of the great works of all time. His genius has been confirmed. He explained and gave order to the heretofore chaotic emerging business system. Smith was to early political economics what Deming is to the Quality Era. Both realized the vital importance of engaging human motivation to achieve business success.

The Motivational Underpinnings of the Market

So widely acclaimed was *The Wealth of Nations* that it eclipsed Smith's earlier thought and writings, from which it had emerged. It has been forgotten by many that Smith had first been a professor of moral philosophy (ethics), a student of human behavior. With remarkable insight into human nature and motivation, his earlier thought, writings, and teaching had focused on the essential aspects of human psychology that activate the instincts to trade and engage in markets and which regulate them once instituted. Most of his theories concerning behavioral motivation and ethical control are contained in his *Theory of Moral Sentiments*, which was published in 1759, (17 years before the appearance of *The Wealth of Nations*). Other concepts are included in notes saved by his students from his instructional series, *Lectures on Police, Justice, Revenue, and Arms*.

For over two centuries now, the focus of modern economists has been to deal with supply-and-demand issues of market growth as well as protection and stimulus. The currently emerging emphasis on quality is a result of maturing markets and informed consumers. Business managers are now realizing through the sharply critical opinions of Deming and others coupled with real-world experiences that scientific management methodology alone cannot move them forward. Progress requires that a more comprehensive understanding of human motivation and interaction be added to the equation.

It is on some of these very philosophical concepts that Adam Smith based *The Wealth of Nations*. We are finding that the Quality Era challenges business motives and ethics. Thankfully, this genius of the 18th century gives us a place to start. The Quality Era, above all, is calling business back from incomplete impersonal concepts of producing, buying, and selling to add fundamental human motivational principles and objectives. Smith's thought began with these concepts and led from there to economics. Businesses and salespeople must reverse this course and go back through economics into its philosophical origins to gain insight for the Quality Era. The course set for Quality Era selling must be charted philosophically. For as business has discovered, narrow behavioral supply and demand models seem to evade essential subjective mechanisms of the market. Thankfully, Adam Smith was a philosopher[3] *first* and an economist second.[10]

There has been in recent times an artificial structuring of disciplines, a compartmentalizing of knowledge into specialized areas—as if these specialties were adequate to stand on their own with little help from other disciplines. Thus a modern business person reaching this point might say, "Let's skip the philosophy and get on with what is needed by business to increase earnings." In Adam Smith's day a philosopher was one who sought to understand the broader mechanisms of nature underlying observed activity. As used in this book, the term "philosophy" means a comprehensive study of the mechanisms that are the foundation of business and market behavior – producing, buying, and selling. One cannot "skip the philosophy" and get on to how to make the money, for to do this is to evade the essence of the issue. As related in Oliver Lodge's introduction to Ruskin's *Unto This Last*, "Abstraction in a science is all very well and is often necessitated by our limited faculties. But abstraction which cuts away essential features and deals with it as if it were the whole is liable to grossly mislead."[11] Modern economics and marketing both risk making this error when they too narrowly define their disciplines. As Ruskin emphasizes, many of the issues of economy operate not mathematically, but *chemically*, thus introducing conditions that render our previous knowledge insufficient. Thus limited, "the reasonings might be admirable, the conclusions true, and the science deficient only in applicability."[12]

The Foundations of the Economy

"Of all animal species only humans truck, barter, and trade," Smith observed.[13] Other animals may appear to cooperate, but this is ultimately instinctive and selfish behavior. What makes this uniquely human ability and bent possible? The keys, Smith determined, were language, which allowed broad interpersonal communication, and a characteristic he called "fellow-feeling", a singular capacity of mankind for sympathetic understanding of our fellow humans. This "fellow-feeling" enables humans to use their imagination to place themselves in another's situation, feeling that person's pain and/or pleasure vicariously.[14] Since humans instinctively sense the feelings of others, this constrains injurious behavior and yields a propriety of conduct that makes possible trust between individuals. Trust alone makes the market possible and, without a degree of trust, civilization is itself impossible. It is this "fellow-feeling" that enables cooperation between people and permits the benefits that flow from it. The concept is essential to selling and to the sales process.

Fellow-Feeling (Empathy)

Smith's "fellow-feeling," which today we would call *empathy*, consists of two facets that he contends allow profitable interaction between human beings. The first is a sense of justice; this sense restrains one individual from doing actual injury to another. Since we humans would "feel" the hurt of others if we should injure them, we normally and naturally refrain from such injury. Smith observes that when we perceive another individual about to be struck by a blow, we wince instinctively in anticipation of the pain, even though it is another who will actually receive the blow.[15]

A second, somewhat higher level of fellow-feeling Smith calls "beneficence." Beneficence is a sense of concern for others and a sense of fair play. Smith observed that humans sympathize with the loss of another's loved one and react with indignation upon seeing another individual shamefully treated.[16] Since we feel and even anticipate hurt when it is about to be inflicted on another, we refrain from behavior that would cause it; thus, a sense of proper behavior results. Because the majority of people possess and react with this sense of propriety based on sentiments of beneficence and justice, trust in social structures and in human interactions such as markets can exist. Some individuals possess so little sense of beneficence that they are cold and callous toward humanity. They may be ostracized and shamed by society, but since they do no overt injury to others they are not subject to actual punishment. Their failure is not in committing injury but in neglecting to help, or to care, when injury has occurred. They make no effort to aid or benefit others through their efforts.[17]

Other individuals lack fellow-feeling to an even deeper extent that allows them to inflict actual injury on others without compassion. These impulses, which lead to injurious actions, are repugnant and intolerable to the mass of society. Such persons must be restrained or set outside of society because they are not restrained by their own sense of justice. Legal systems are established by society to accomplish this purpose, and, according to Smith, this is a primary reason for the establishment of governmental justice.[18] Injury, or transgressing the public sense of justice, can be physical, financial, or reputational. Empathy is therefore a most powerful human characteristic, one whose lack necessitates government and whose prevailing presence enables trade to exist through restraint of unbridled selfish impulse. Empathy has overriding importance for business leadership and selling, yet this vital concept is found rarely, if at all, in the topical indexes of modern management, economics, or marketing texts.

Self-Interest

Smith observed that all humans are motivated by self-interest and that their activities are rooted in it.[19] He remarked that in the market (selling) one instinctively attempts to persuade others to buy his product through appeal to the customer's self-interest. "Man . . . works on the self love of his fellows by setting before them a sufficient temptation to get what he wants. . . . No one but a beggar expects to be given something except from appeal to his own self-interest."[20] Smith thus identified the chief motivating force of the human race as perceived self-interest. *Individual effort fueled by self-interest, yet restrained by a sense of beneficence and justice, is the underpinning of the economy and of modern society itself.*

Smith observed that the motivation of self-interest enabled in the workplace produced measurable differences in productivity between free laborers and slaves. Mines on one side of a mountain range between Turkey and Hungary were worked on the Turkish side by slaves and on the Hungarian side by "free," or paid, labor. The production of the free laborers was much greater than that of the slave labor although other factors were equal.[21]

The motivating power of self-interest has proven itself to be enormous through the results produced by the world's free economies as contrasted to those not so enabled. Smith observed that the slave's only motivation is fear of punishment; no positive individual results are achieved from added effort. "Therefore, the slave does only what he is told and brings no creativity or ingenuity to his work."[22] Deming says we must eliminate fear to enable quality in work.[4] Smith, too, notes that fear stifles creativity and initiative. He observed that in nations where "the manufacturers were carried out by slaves, they were not carried on so well as by freemen and thus those nations showed slow progress of arts and commerce."[23] Modern business should listen.

Empathy in Business and Sales

Smith's fellow-feeling restrains the normal self-interest that motivates all men and women. When so constrained, self-interest motivates and guides business activity so that it is productive for the individual as well as for society, allowing social harmony and order to be preserved. Consider also that the sense of empathy that allows us to feel the pain or pleasure of others through empathetic projection can also allow us to anticipate another individual's reaction to a concept, product, or to a price. It is this unheralded empathetic characteristic that has guided man from the beginning in the design and production of products and services that become a delight to customers. Does it not assist also in developing price structures that will seem "reasonable" in relation to value?

The company, whose management and sales personnel would understand the attitudes and desires of the customer public, must use empathy to guide the development of products and sales relationships and thus win customer loyalty in the marketplace of the Quality Era. Is it not apparent that genuine care and concern (guided by empathy) taken in the production and service of products can come through to the delight of the customer? The Quality Era will belong not to the customer survey statistician but to the empathetic. Each business person represents an empathetic model of the customer. Business managers and salespeople must cultivate and use a heightened empathetic sense acquired through close personal dealings with others. Statistical knowledge can be used to verify empathetic understanding but not replace it.

In reality, it is empathetic understanding that business must seek from the statistics. This is what Deming and other Quality Era authorities mean by important business numbers being unknown and unknowable. Empathy is the context through which Quality Era managers will dialog with employees and, subsequently, salespeople will dialog with customers. Empathy is the antithesis of a cold and distant relationship with either employees or customers. In fact, Smith notes that the empathetic sense is diminished as distance increases, but "more readily assumes the shape and configuration of those with whom I am familiar."[24]

Humankind – The Dissatisfied Animal

What underlies the self-interest motivation in mankind? Smith observes that man is the "dissatisfied" animal that seems unable to use anything in its natural state: food must be cooked, clothing woven and sewn, houses built, and so forth. Humans are self-driven to seek continual betterment in each of these areas and more. Given a house, they want a better one; given clothing, they want something finer. Of all the species on earth, only the human can be offended by the color and arrangement of items.[25] Smith goes on to say, our continual search for a greater degree of nicety takes up most of our time where the bare essentials could be obtained with much less effort and time. This may not be how we would wish to be, but this is how we are. This is the impetus of the market. Smith, perhaps above all others, legitimated the profit motive as a modus that benefits society. Through his writing, business and selling gained moral support and new acceptance.

Smith contemplated many facets of the concept of value.

"We place a great value on items of unique beauty but little practical use, such as jewels," he commented. Smith noted that when early explorers of the Americas traded glass "jewels" of larger size to the natives for real jewels of smaller scale, the natives hid in fear that the explorers would want to reverse what had obviously been a bad trade.[26] Issues of value and taste vary from person to person and moment to moment and depend on each individual's own perspective on utility, beauty, and scarcity.

Smith saw that if the economic mechanisms of nations and individuals were to be governed and encouraged for maximum overall benefit, they had to be based on philosophically sound principles that were in tune with the realities of the natural order. As the impact of the Industrial Revolution created its impact of greater availability and lower cost, an explosion of choices became available. The dramatic expansion of economies that has occurred over the last 200 years has diverted business toward a narrow focus on how to manage success and maximize profit. This time may well be seen by future generations as a distinct aberration in the overall history of the market.

The diversity of choice available to the customer in the emerging global marketplace increasingly makes it a buyer's market. The correct conceptual perspective of quality, value, and empathy must once again guide business in the Quality Era. Smith and other writers have given us useful insights, but many of their writings that focus on quality markets are found in the library not under "economics" but under "social philosophy," "ethics," and even "art criticism." Quality Era selling philosophy requires turning from an excessively narrow economic theory toward a much broader, more synergistic one where the *attitudinal* aspects of producing, buying, and selling receive a new and appropriate emphasis.

John Ruskin

Great fortunes were made when modern technology was applied to fulfilling the market demands of the 18th and 19th centuries. Writers other than Adam Smith contributed concepts relevant to the approaching Quality Era. John Ruskin, an English art critic, became interested in economics through his deliberations on the differing values in art and architecture. Some of his thoughts could almost be taken from Deming's Quality concepts. For example:

- It should be the art (i.e., the design quality) in a thing that we purchase.[27]
- We should seek items produced by happy workers.[28]
- The most important factors of economics are *chemical* and not *mathematical*[29]; they cannot be counted numerically. (Compare this statement to Deming's contention that the business community shouldn't attempt to reduce buyer behavior to statistics alone – more is at work, and such behavior is constantly changing.)

If we use modern terms for those of Ruskin's day, we find him saying that "design and production quality" is what customers are buying, that joy in work is a key to worker interest and better products, and that the work atmosphere and the intangible motivational aspects of a business are often the most essential ingredients in approaching quality performance. These are often the factors that, as Deming suggests, "are unknown and often unknowable as numerical data."[30] We can also observe that the phrase "chemical, not numerical" can imply emotional factors, not just rational ones. Ruskin stresses that management must enlist the *affections* (i.e., the commitment) of workers.[31]

Ruskin's observations point toward an ethical and socially positive philosophy of business. They lead away from the purely numerical and toward attitudes of management's responsibility and duty to customers. In this observant critic, Deming and other architects of the modern Quality Era can find considerable historical support. Business must add the subjective to the objective to gain comprehensive understanding.

Early Discussions of Value

Ruskin also considered the essential question, "What is value?" His conclusion was that value must essentially be utility or

27

usefulness in its broadest sense. He went on to build on an earlier definition of wealth offered by a contemporary philosopher, John Stuart Mill, who had said that wealth consisted in "the possession of many things that have value (usefulness) in situations of exchange." Ruskin contended that an item is valuable to its owner to the degree that it is personally useful. Therefore, he concluded, "Wealth is the possession of many *useful* things."[32]

Very valuable modern insights can flow from this perspective. Customer education and training in using and appreciating the product can actually increase overall value. A product is of most use or value to its owner when it is capable of being used and appreciated fully. This has implications for the education, skill requirements, support, reliability, and longevity provided in products. Clearly, all of a product's value does not reside within the product itself; it is also affected by the readiness of the customer to receive, use, and enjoy it.

This concept has broader implications. In any selling situation, the customer trades an item of less use for one of more use (i.e., value) to him. The same is true for the vendor who has an excess of product and a need for added money. If wealth is "the possession of useful things," each market transaction can produce increased wealth for both buyer and seller. Both win. Trade itself "creates" increased individual wealth. Philosophically, wealth may be infinitely available as new information and technology, combined with ingenuity, make more raw materials increasingly more "useful" and as more richness and variety in trade ensues.

Ruskin also seems to foresee pertinent ethical questions of the Quality Era when he cites Alexander Pope, a contemporary who observed, "An honest man is one of God's greatest works now apparent, and somewhat a rare one." Ruskin defends this statement with regard to honesty in business dealings with employees and customers. According to Ruskin, many will criticize simple honesty as too modest a goal. He counters, "It may well be enough, for honesty alone allows business to proceed free of chaos!"[33]

This discourse advocates the attitude of fairness in trade and solid value delivered in products as well as the honest encouragement and support of workers. The period in which Ruskin lived saw great exploitation of workers by business owners who were driven by what the public perceived as obvious greed. It was in this era that capitalists earned a bad reputation and social reformers, such as Ruskin, began to point out that this unbridled self-interest was counterproductive to societal good. A workplace atmosphere that evokes trust and encourages workers' self-worth is very much a part of the Quality Era concept. Honesty in selling and in business also means setting realistic expectations for products and consistently meeting or exceeding them as they are perceived by our customers.

Selling

"Selling" as a concept of pushing goods toward consumers and of seeking out customers directly is somewhat an American exclusive. The growth and expansion of the United States stimulated entrepreneurial efforts, and sales and selling were a part of that boom. People's dreams of products shown by traveling salespeople penetrated the isolation and monotony of early America and stimulated the desires of its people. Such dreams motivated, but sometimes the product reality disillusioned. These salespeople were products of their times and would be inadequate in the marketplace of today. Europeans were generally more reserved in "offering" products in the market. The Pacific Rim nations had not yet awakened.

Over the last 50 years trade, motivated through sales promotion and marketing, has continued to stimulate the desires of mankind. Selling, both personal and impersonal (through advertising), now stimulates the search for betterment among all the peoples of the global marketplace. The human race, thus motivated, has arrived at this new era of broadest market competition in which issues of quality and perceived value have become the criteria for business success.

It can appear wasteful for businesses offering similar products to compete in a free market. A planned and organized central selection process might choose and plan what is to be produced and offered to the market; this would eliminate the need for selling. The great amounts of capital expended competing through appeals to customer desires could then apparently be spent on increased production or lower pricing. What is not so apparent, but borne out in experience, is that the productive efficiencies and energies derived from free business competition in pursuit of self-interest overwhelm its apparent inefficiencies. The test has been made in the real-world arena, and nations are turning toward free market economic strategy as the best hope for their people. No altruistic motivation seems able to approach self-interest as a motivator of human productivity.

Selling and competitive marketing are unique components of free enterprise. Indeed, knowledge of what customers want, as evidenced by what they buy in a free market, is a most valuable information feedback mechanism that constantly tunes product design and production. Salespeople can help society dream of better things; the resulting demand leads business to produce and deliver them. It should only be required that producing and selling be conducted with integrity and societal responsibility. As we shall see, the Quality Era will demand it. Empathetic insight and concern for customer delight through quality and value of product is the new guiding principle.

The drive for opulence and self-interest has been unleashed by innovation and invention; thus enabled, it has reached its current level of expression. The new quality philosophy injects an experiential wholesomeness into the process, giving higher purpose to business and higher quality to customers.

Summary

The instinct to trade is as old as the human race. It is driven by a desire to better one's condition enabled by language and empathy, which allow us to imaginatively estimate the needs of others and to communicate to them about goods or services that might answer those needs. The market is a situation or place that allows for the exchange of goods or services.

Humans desire goods or services based on how they perceive that these goods or services fit their needs and how efficiently they can be obtained. Thus the concept of value perception based on the ratio of usefulness to cost is the decision criterion in the market. The discussion of value and attention to it was in earlier times instigated by merchants and traders; in more recent times, it has been championed by salespeople.

Over the last few hundred years, an unprecedented explosion of goods and services has been made available in the market as science and technology are incorporated efficiently into products. These products are increasingly of uniquely excellent design, causing a shift in emphasis from sellers who control a tight supply to buyers who demand excellence or quality. The ability to produce excellence in a product and to communicate it to customers is becoming a pivotal issue in what is becoming a world marketplace. The issue is made doubly complex because "quality" in product demands thoughtful commitment by producers and leadership by management – that is, there is a motivational and perceptive dimension that must be added to elevate products to the new levels of excellence demanded by the market. Addressing these philosophical issues as outlined by Deming and, in an earlier time, by Ruskin and Smith will prove to be the great challenge of businesses and salespeople in this new Quality Era.

References

[1] Neave, H. R., 1990. *The Deming Dimension*. Knoxville, TN: SPC Press, p. 26 – 27.

[2] Ibid, p. 34.

[3] Deming, W. Edwards, 1986. *Out of the Crisis*. Cambridge, MA: MIT Press, pp. 23 – 24.

[4] Smith, Adam, 1982. *Lectures on Jurisprudence,* Liberty Classics: Indianapolis, p. 367.

[5] Heilbroner, Robert L., 1986. *The Worldly Philosophers*. New York: Simon and Schuster, p. 21.

[6] Ibid, p. 23.

[7] Ibid, p. 25

[8] Durant, Will and Ariel, 1961. *The Age of Reason*. New York: Simon and Schuster, pp. 184 – 185.

[9] Smith, *Lectures*, 224, 526.

[10] Smith, Adam, 1982. *Essays on Philosophical Subjects*. Indianapolis: Liberty Classics, p. 13 – 14.

[11] Ruskin, John, 1907. *Unto This Last.* London: J. M. Dent & Sons, Ltd., p. *ix.*

[12] Ibid, p. 115 – 116.

[13] Smith, Adam, (1776) 1952. *An Inquiry into the Nature and Causes of the Wealth of Nations.* Chicago: Encyclopedia Britannica Great Books.

[14] Smith, Adam, (1759), 1982. *The Theory of Moral Sentiments.* Indianapolis: Liberty Fund, p. 9.

[15] Ibid, p. 9, 29.

[16] Ibid, p. 79.

[17] Ibid, p. 78 – 79

[18] Ibid, p. 86 – 87

[19] Ibid, pp. 82 – 83.

[20] Smith, *Wealth of Nations,* p. 7

[21] Smith, *Wealth of Nations,* p. 299

[22] Smith, *Wealth of Nations,* p. 298 – 299

[23] Smith, *Lectures,* p. 521 – 53

[24] Smith, *Moral Sentiments,* p. 24

[25] Smith, *Lectures,* (Liberty Fund Edition) pp. 334 – 335.

[26] Ibid, p. 336.

[27] Ruskin, John, 1907. *Unto This Last.* London: J. M. Dent & Sons, Ltd., p. 64.

[28] Ruskin, John, 1891. *Lectures on Archetecture and Painting.* London: George Allen, p. 83.

[29] Ruskin, *Unto This Last.* p. 115

[30] Neave, *The Deming Dimension,* p. 151.

[31] Ruskin, *Unto This Last.* p. 119.

[32] Ibid, p. 165.

[33] Ibid, p. 110.

Notes

1. Dr. Deming made this observation in a 1988 seminar held in Denver, Colorado.

2. The full title of this work is *An Inquiry into the Nature and Causes of the Wealth of Nations,* commonly refered to today as *The Wealth of Nations.*

3. Smith defined philosophy as "the science of the connecting principles of nature." Thus, a "philosopher" of Smith's day was a scientist studying natural order. The word "scientist" did not exist before 1839.

4. See Deming's point 8.

CHAPTER 2

THE NEW MARKETPLACE

What is the Same

The modern global marketplace can seem complex and even chaotic, but many of its essential elements have been present throughout history. The human dissatisfaction with present condition and the desire for betterment observed by Adam Smith still fuel the engine of the economic system. The economies of entire nations are enabled for economic competition to the degree that their societies provide stable political structure for markets. Societies that respect and engender justice and beneficence within their populations have the advantage. Everyone is at times either a buyer or a seller, and each person possesses a capacity for empathetic understanding of the other position. The most effective businesses and salespeople act empathetically toward customers.

The market has always been competitive – even from the time that two or more sources of supply became available for a product – and in the beginning the customer already represented one source of supply. If a baker's bread, or a butcher's meat, were not of sufficient quality, customers had the option to produce their own. Only as expertise or specialization of labor produced a sufficient quality of product at an acceptable price could an item gain market viability. That relationship between the usefulness of an item or service and its price came to be called "value," and the customer of today still searches for products with the most usefulness at the lowest cost. This concept of value is perceived in very individualized and personal terms by each customer.

Today's customer shops in a much larger marketplace. In earlier times, competition was constrained by isolation; this allowed local businesses the luxury of being literally "the only game in town." Today, the town is the world. With global communication of product advantage and rapid – even overnight – delivery upon purchase, the best products can enjoy literally worldwide success; the less good can die quickly. The new marketplace opens up wide opportunities to more specialized vendor products. The global market is comprised of many people having highly diverse and individualized needs. Vendors can develop products targeted at these highly specific customer needs and promote their sale through precise marketing channels. For example, over 50 years ago, magazines appeared in the United States published solely for physicians. About ten years ago, a magazine appeared that targeted female physicians. Recently, a magazine was introduced that targeted female physicians having personal interest in health and fitness, a still smaller and more specific group. The media and methods available for reaching increasingly specific groups with a product message have increased dramatically. The ability to relate customer demographics to product capability is one of the great new marketing forces of the Quality Era. The process is facilitated by information technology undreamed of in the past. The Quality Era is the era of precise, targeted selling.

Because the world is now the marketplace, highly specialized products can draw sufficient customers from increasingly vast geographic areas until a vendor's target customer set can encompass the globe. Communications and information technology are breaking through the barriers that tended to keep products undifferentiated and within restricted geography due to an inability to communicate with the number of customers required for specialized markets. The trends toward specialization of product and targeted appeals to highly specific audiences will continue to grow and become more efficient. Based on this trend and the increasing ability to target highly specialized customers with customized products, the sales volumes of many general-purpose product vendors and of less innovative companies will be eroded. Potential sales volumes of increasingly specific products are becoming sufficient to support highly specialized businesses.

In the midst of this promotion of specialized products to target audiences, there is a great background of "noise." The issue for customers is becoming: "What is the most suitable product for my needs?" and "How do I find it against a backdrop of increasing market noise?" The global marketplace is enormous, with vendors at every hand crying, "Buy this!" and "Buy it here!" The customer can feel that there are too many choices, and the meaning of value and quality are confused by the varied array of offerings, approaches, and even distortion of facts.

This is occurring in the face of an increasing number of buying decisions being made by customers on a daily basis. Almost too much information is being pushed toward the customer for conscious consideration, much less logical processing. What was to have been the Information Age has the potential of becoming the Misinformation Age. Confusion can appear to reign. Drenched with information, customers feel bewildered. They are beginning to search for safe havens represented by products and by vendors that can be depended upon and that allow a respite from the clamor of the marketplace.

Two stages of customer approval are clearly emerging. The first involves considering several vendors or products; the second is selecting one product or vendor from those under consideration. Many vendors and their products will not be considered and will therefore have no chance of being selected. In self defense, customers are limiting vendor access to their consciousness. To be included in the group being considered is becoming a challenge in Quality Era selling.

The product and vendor reputations from the older market era expanded with trademarks and brand names. The product is endorsed by the manufacturer's seal on the label, suggesting to the customer that since an historically reputable company has its trademark on the product, the product will be as good as the company that produces it. Even this rationale, though true in many cases, has been distorted by the acquisition of companies with reputations for quality by firms that capitalize on previously superior brand names and issue products of diminished quality. The customer's quest is still for value – quality at reasonable price. The search is becoming more complicated.

The overriding characteristic of the new marketplace is, above all, its size. The world is becoming one marketplace. In this new market, to remain competitive – to make and sell products that customers want to buy – empathy must play a guiding role. The future will belong to the company that best understands the concerns of the customer and uses that understanding to guide product design, to direct its product message, and to structure its subsequent service after a sale is made. The decision to buy is still, and will always be, made in the mind of each customer. Success lies in emphatically meeting and exceeding the expectations of the customer mind. Quality Era vendors must establish a new level of empathetic identity with their customers. Vendors will themselves assist customers in setting increasingly higher expectations of product performance – all of this with concern for the national, ethnic, cultural, and geographical diversity of the new marketplace. There is, however, no composite customer mind, only individual customer minds with essential, common aspects.

The innovations that are producing the new global marketplace are, in essence, the result of the creation of new tools. Tools enhance basic human capabilities, enabling a level of performance of tasks that would be impossible without them. The understanding that it is the tools that are new, and not the fundamentals, can give great comfort when we attempt to understand the changing world around us. Tools can only enable strategy; they cannot create it.

Though vendors and customers maintain the same impulses and attitudes described by Adam Smith in the 1700s, the ability to make our voices heard (via telephone); our writing read (via printing); ourselves and our products visible (via photographs, videotape, teleconferencing, and television); and, of course, our products and even ourselves present (via high-speed transportation), we are still confined to the village. If a village consists of those with whom one is in daily contact, discussion, interaction, association, dialogue, and trade, the new tools have made this possible on a global scale. The village has become global.

The new tools allow us to consult and access evaluations of product performance with a sophistication unknown in earlier times. Increasing numbers of businesses make use of consulting experts to help make intelligent buying decisions. Even home buyers now often pay agents to assist them in obtaining the "perfect" new home. Increasingly, customers are seeking information from product tests and evaluations through such publications as *Consumer Reports*. These tools supplement the customer's impressions of product quality and value. They are each forms of an empathetic product evaluation being performed so that the customer can estimate the potential value of the product. The methodology of payment has diverged from barter and relatively scarce coinage to plentiful bank notes. Payment methodologies now include instant loans through credit cards and bank credit lines. Payment transcends national borders and offers ready exchange, for nominal fees, among world currencies. These tools make it easier for the customer to buy; they have replaced old barriers. They facilitate selling.

International Implications

The impact of the global marketplace in world affairs cannot be overstated. In the earlier phases of the current economic revolution, issues of trade and economics precipitated military conflict. In the current era, world leaders have come to recognize that the new stage of national status and prosperity does not rest so much on military strength as it did in the past. Today, national strength rests largely on the ability of a nation to develop and produce for trade products with wide appeal in the world marketplace. Nations must also offer a certain quality of life to their own citizens, who have now become aware of the lifestyles and quality products available in other nations.

Japan, which was essentially destroyed after World War II, is today an economic powerhouse with enormous wealth and technological strength, all developed while renouncing military force. The Japanese realized they had been beaten by superior production and technology; they subsequently committed to a new national strategy totally economic and without military option. The results of that decision are evident.

The Soviet Union, once feared as one of the world's great superpowers, has crumbled because it could not compete economically and technologically in the emerging world marketplace. Its people, hungry for the consumer goods of the West and the better life offered by free economies, ousted their old leaders. Now they are attempting to establish a market economy.

The question for nations who are behind, such as Russia, is not whether to play in the global economy but whether they can catch up in order to become true players. The resources of a rich infrastructure, such as transportation, information, technology, education, and financial systems, all act synergistically to form a critical mass that can propel some nations far ahead of others in their capability to bring product value into the changing world marketplace. Missing ingredients can cost dearly. Russia and the emerging nations of the Third World have enormous gaps to bridge if their products are to reach world-class quality and value status. Those nations that are ahead in this competition will not slow their pace but will accelerate it as aggregate internal capabilities enable even greater capability.

Customer Changes

Customers within the new global marketplace are better educated than those of the past. Public education is a recent, but now almost worldwide, reality. Educated individuals are more discriminating buyers, more value-conscious. This ratio of cost to utility is increasingly being considered and presented on more sophisticated levels.

Products are no longer being considered only on their basic functional characteristics; durability, longevity, and serviceability are considered value factors also. Customers now frequently study products from a systems standpoint. They may seek products that offer an implementation and support structure that ensures that the total functional expectations of the product are achieved. This requires vendors to provide enhanced support such as comprehensive training for operators who, when thoroughly informed about products, can help customers get the most benefit from them. It can also mean fool-proof products that do the proper things automatically and thus ensure success and satisfaction.

Customers are increasingly focused on the safety aspects of

product design so that occasional, extraneous, negative results are eliminated. Safety considerations are a part of environmental impact considerations, all of which are of importance to growing numbers of customers. The legal implications of product misusage or of functional failure plague product manufacturers and vendors as well.

Sophisticated customers are expecting reliable, positive service from products that have no negatives. Competition is forcing producers to either deliver performance at these new levels or fall behind. Equipment failure rates in certain devices, including computer equipment, are approaching a point where failure is not to be expected on any component during the useful life of the machine. More and more products will be replaced because of functional obsolescence, not because they will not function at all.

The customer is often in a hurry and challenged on all sides for his or her attention. Disillusioned customers can become suspicious, expecting vendors to be overstating benefits and performance of products. This suspicion has to be overcome in order to earn traditional supplier status. Even when a vendor or product manufacturer has done everything and produced a product that meets the requirements of function and reliability, with high quality and strong value, it may fail in the marketplace simply because it lacks style or fashion appeal. Customers can be fickle. If a company does not understand which personality aspects customers wish to express through a product type, its products may not sell. Adam Smith observed that most businesses take too small a view of risk. The risks in this new economy are more real than ever. Not understanding the customer is possibly the greatest risk.

Observation of customer behavior indicates a strong desire to identify reliable and convenient sources of product and services. The intensity of activity has increased, and the time available for each decision has been reduced. The more automated decisions can become regarding certain purchases, the more time is available to evaluate other decisions in depth. Thus, the rapid pace of life and the persuasive noise coming from all sides will drive customers to select standard sources for their purchases.

The concept of a "safe harbor" is not an inaccurate analogy for this trend. Having a safe harbor relieves customer stress produced by the necessity of a continual search for new sources and new products. Without it, the customer must deal with the unfamiliar and the untried. New locales and new personalities must be encountered, all of which can be more stressful and time-consuming than buying the known and familiar.

The challenge is to become that known and familiar source of product to which customers turn out of habit and familiarity. There is in this challenge the hope that if reliable sources of reliable product can be found for all the necessities of life, there will be more leisure time. The desire is to simplify life, but the elimination of all buying stress is probably not really attainable.

The customers of today, from the consumer of household products to the individual buying for large businesses, are seeking reliable "purchase points" they can trust. Relationships between the customer and the vendor are built on the general characteristics of dependable product function and surrounding service, on the overall quality of the product, on the convenience of doing business with the vendor, and on a less tangible but equally important factor: the attitude and atmosphere of the vendor's company. In the mind of the customer, vendor companies acquire an image that equates to a personality. The building and maintaining of the right personality as perceived by customers is one of the great challenges to business and to salespeople of the Quality Era.

These traditional product source relationships save time in decision-making; they may also save money as well. Such a relationship may be based on a recognition of traditional low cost. Special pricing, rebates, as well as perk credits (e.g., frequent flyer programs, coupons, free service, and the like), may also be available to traditional customers. The customer may also have hope that special relationships will pay off when a crisis or need for special service occurs – that such vendors will make an extraordinary effort to fulfill a unique customer need. This additional security has value. In addition, there can be less worry over product quality and reliability because there is an expectation that a product sold by a trusted vendor would not be offered by them unless it were also trustworthy and that any failure will be remedied. Many vendors now even pretest products they offer, but do not manufacture, to ensure quality performance for their customers.

Reputation for Quality

Both vendor name and reputation and brand name and reputation help to eliminate concern about actual product performance and about the risk of an unsatisfactory outcome. Customers will often pay more for a brand-name item than for a generic product, but they may trust a generic item more because it is offered by a vendor they trust. You can visualize the range of this phenomenon by using a wristwatch as an example. The greatest confidence might be in a brand-name watch sold by a highly reputable jeweler, and the least confidence in a unknown person who approaches you on the subway to sell you a watch of unknown make. Somewhere in between would be an unfamiliar watch sold by a reputable jeweler.

Product source relationships are of crucial importance today and will be of great importance in the future. From the vendor's standpoint, product sales subsequent to the first can require much less effort and expense because a basis of trust, familiarity, and information has already been established. The hope for a continued satisfactory relationship built on ongoing purchases and sales and a history of positive experiences becomes a defense against an occasion in which performance is not up to expectation. The first sale can be the most difficult, but subsequent sales should become less so and therefore more efficient for the vendor as well as for the customer. Quality Era sales personnel must develop these product source relationships with diligence. They should be established and maintained by careful attention to service and customer issues.

The Quality Era sales group should become a conduit for customer input to the vendor, thus producing a visible improvement of products, service, and policy. If properly built, these relationships become almost an annuity for the vendor and a point of convenience for the customer that neither will wish to break. Ultimately, a customer may become familiar with vendor procedures and products to the point that they become their own salesperson. A customer who is thoroughly knowledgeable about a vendor's organization and procedures can do much of his or her own work in the buying process when they perceive that time or service can be gained. This knowledgeable buyer requires less time on the part of vendor salespeople, other departments, and, in general, can be the most productive type of customer. These loyal customers will also "work" for the vendor's company in advising and selling others concerning the vendor's products. In the interest of saving their own time and money, many customers will select their own merchandise, pick up their own order at a vendor location, and so forth. One remarkable modern phenomenon is that of the fast-food customers who clear their own tables when they leave a restaurant.

A study of the expense-to-value ratio of the customer relationship pattern from the development of the first sale to a traditional product source status would show how attaining such a status with a customer would greatly increase the vendor's efficiency. It might also show why added effort on the front end at the point of first sale is worth the expense and effort. It has been estimated that it costs a vendor up to five times as much to create a new customer as to keep an old one.

Motivational Consequences

Motivation and compensation plans for sales personnel are beginning to be developed with this long-range customer-creation view in mind. It is interesting that most insurance companies have long structured their compensation plans along lines that pay the agent an annuity-type commission for an ongoing policy relationship and not just a front-end sales bonus. Such incentive plans can help produce the perspective required to work toward relationship building rather than the "get the order and run" mentality that was all too common in the past and, some may comment, is still prevalent.

IBM, in its early growth phase, paid its salespeople on a net rental revenue increase basis. Salespeople were paid to increase territory revenue of rental customers and were debited if customers canceled rental for competitor equipment; thus the incentive was constant to keep present customers happy and to sell properly to new ones. Sales that did not "stick" cost the salespeople time and effort and netted them nothing. Since management gets the behavior that it encourages, motivational programs should be tied to the type of sale a company really wants to make.

Innovations in technology can make possible an atmosphere of enhanced personalization if used properly. It is tragic that many companies make such poor use of information technology in this regard. One often hears that the reason for a delay at a sales counter or a bank teller window is "the computer is down" or "the computer won't let us do that." This creates a false attitude that computerization means impersonalization. Management planning and proper system design can use the new information technology to enhance greatly the perception of the personal touch in dealing with customers. This personalization makes customers feel better known and understood – "a personality," a name, not a number. Ultimately, people enjoy dealing personality to personality with others and feeling that they are a "preferred," or "special," customer. The objective must be to build personalized relationships. Automation can be of great assistance if management understands and creatively designs and directs the use of technology toward personalized dealings with the customer. Businesses that take this approach can have dramatic success in the global marketplace. Their competition may not even suspect how much business advantage they enjoy. The following examples point out how modern information technology can secure customer loyalty. As Deming noted, success is shown when customers return again and again and again.

An Example

Anyone outside the IBM Corporation would be amazed at the number of pairs of relatively high-priced shoes that have been sold nationwide to IBM executives and salespeople by a small shoe store in Pontotoc, Mississippi. These are, for the most part, top of the line items produced by Florsheim and Allen-Edmonds, two of the more expensive lines of men's shoes. Many are shell cordovan tasseled loafers and wing tips averaging $250 or more per pair. The Progressive Shoe Store has become the traditional product source for shoes for a great many individuals throughout the United States by giving excellent value and service and by building relationships with a specific set of customers for high price-point merchandise.

What are some of the characteristics that make this situation work for both the vendor and the customer? Possibly the chief reason for buying from Progressive is convenience. Progressive Shoe deals with a business customer set that is not often willing to take time out to go shopping for shoes. Second, it has a clear picture of the products its customers want to buy, which are often the same styles and brands they have been buying for years. Progressive does not stock all of the sizes and styles available but rather has implemented a very quick drop-shipment approach that allows the company to keep inventory investment low. Because the cost of operation, including inventory, is low, savings are produced that can be shared by customer and vendor. This means about a 20- to 25-percent savings to the customer over regular retail price for the items involved, but the quality and service are still excellent. The message about this company as a product source has spread over time throughout the IBM Corporation by customer selling customer, and it continues to grow on this base of success. As this example illustrates, the advertising for a traditional source is often satisfied customers who tell others. Progressive supplements this with occasional direct mail of manufacturer brochures plus a price list – a very low-cost and efficient type of advertising that contributes further to their price advantage.

If I, as a past customer of Progressive, call their number, a friendly voice answers: "This is Tammy. May I help you?" I give my name and mention a desired brand and style, and Tammy gives me the current price. She comments that my last order was in July of 1994 and asks me if I was pleased with that order. She "knows" my shoe size, the styles I have bought in the past, my credit card number, my shipping address, and an estimated delivery date (usually within a week) for my order. I am not required to repeat the basic information but only to indicate what I want. The transaction is quick and convenient, faster by far than leaving home or office to shop and much cheaper and hassle-free. This is service geared to my needs, and unless there is some major problem with this vendor or products it will remain my traditional product source for shoes.

Tammy's knowledge of my buying history and other data comes, of course, from a customer-oriented database and computer display terminal that places my personal information in front of her based on any one of several search codes, including last name, zip code, and so forth. Systems are now available that recognize the calling customer's phone number and can bring up the required customer information before a word is spoken by either party. Conversation is carried on with an apparent personal knowledge of the customer on the part of the vendor, a real key to hassle-free shopping. Of course, there was a first time when basic information had to be recorded, but from then on only new information needed entry. Subsequent orders build the history. The history can be monitored to follow the relationship.

Should Progressive wish to advertise a sale on a particular style of shoe, it might select customers who have purchased that style in the past or those who have not. The company's computer could be linked to the manufacturer and the order transmitted for drop shipment immediately upon hanging up the phone. Inventory to be actually stocked could be evaluated based on size and style information regarding the buying history of all customers and the anticipated demand based on that history. The information is available and so is the technology. Only the creativity of management sets the limits for its use. Another option, perhaps, might be a review of the average life of a style of shoe and a call or letter at a point just prior to "wear out" advising buyers of that type of shoe that they are due for another pair, similar to the oil-change reminders sent by auto dealers. The possibilities are unlimited. Progressive is not a shoe store; it is a footwear-providing *system* that meets some customer's needs more efficiently than a traditional shoe store.

A Two-Way Understanding

The key to designing and using systems that will build the traditional product source relationship in the Quality Era will be the creativity and commitment of management and customer insight provided through empathy. Successful business managers today must understand the attitudes and emotions of their customers. As current literature on quality is pointing out, customers may not know all they might want or be able to get in a product or service; empathetic design of product and structure of service should mean advancing into designs that anticipate what the customer might want and possibly will demand tomorrow.

Competitors will be taking similar steps. The prize can be business success on a global scale. Failure to understand the mind of customers and anticipate their needs can mean business decline. Businesses must develop an increasing awareness of comprehensive product possibilities that might be made available: why customers might appreciate them, what frustrations are produced by lack of these features, what such products or features should cost, and how they should look. This is visionary market leadership. Empathetic understanding of customers must reach up to vendor management because only management can implement the companywide approaches required by the Quality Era.

Such empathetic understanding cannot be obtained exclusively from statistical data or past performance. An excessive reliance on past statistics is similar to steering an auto by looking in the rear-view mirror. Statistics tend to tell how much happened but not why. The "why" is key, for trends and currents of customer behavior change rapidly. Windows of product opportunity open and close much more quickly in today's marketplace. Statistics are cold, without feeling, and do not address issues at the individual level.

Customer attitudes must be empathetically perceived by the company. Products and comprehensive services must then be brought rapidly into line with changing customer desires. Success lies not just in being led by the customer; business must establish leadership by showing customers what products can be improved and then communicate the meaning of these innovations in terms of product enjoyment. Improvements in product and service must flow continuously toward the customer as quickly as they can be identified and implemented. The ability to innovate rapidly in a process of continual quality improvement can give strong advantages to small companies that lack the bureaucratic inertia of larger firms. Many larger firms are organizing into smaller, dedicated, independent divisions in order to gain market responsiveness.

The Sales Group Can Do More Than Sell

Since empathetic guidance of company strategy is essential to success, those groups within the business organization with the greatest focus on direct customer interaction must effectively provide insight into customer attitudes and feelings to managers who are capable of altering strategy. Usually the front line of customer contact is the sales group. Their effectiveness in selling is based on an understanding of the customers' prevailing attitudes. Top management cannot assume that it is hearing the customer's voice through the sales organization simply because periodic reviews are held with the marketing group or with sales management.

Communications are often filtered upward in organizations, and this filtering takes its toll. Exclusive high-level executive exposure is coveted by mid-level management. Empathy and sensitivity for customer issues may not be factors that lead to a mid-level manager's rise in an organization. The response of headquarters to bad news can be, "Shoot the messenger!" The organizational structure itself can serve to hamper vital information flow upward. New structures must be put in place by which not only field sales input but customer input gain immediate access to high-level management. In the relationship building that must take place in the Quality Era, the customers who make a business their traditional product source must be actively engaged to keep a check on the success of the vendor's products and policies. Every policy and product must be gauged by its effect as perceived by the customer.

The picture of the future is one of salespeople and customers rapidly supplying performance and attitudinal information back to the vendor company regarding reaction to product, policies, and new needs. This information flow needs to occur freely, to be available constantly, and to be heard daily by top management. It should continuously influence both operations and strategy. Input from both customers and sales regarding competitive moves and innovations must be transmitted as well. Dr. Deming proposed such a feedback loop often referred to as the "Deming Cycle" or "PDCA Cycle." Through this concept he stressed the importance of constant interaction among research, design, production, and sales in order for a company to arrive at better quality, which satisfies customers.

Excessive formality must be eliminated. Information needs to be in useful form, but the traditional corporate requirement for approaching internal executives through a hierarchical strategy, with presentations at increasingly higher levels, not only filters information but often alters its basic thrust. Political forces are at work in vendor organizations, and intervening levels of middle management know that bringing top management bad news or unplanned results can be bad strategy politically.

If organizations are to prosper, truth and openness at all levels is essential. This is asking a great deal, for modern business can take on the form of interdepartmental warfare, and it has been said that "in war, the first casualty is truth."

One quite remarkable breakthrough in business communications that can facilitate transparent reporting of facts upward is internal electronic mail (e-mail). In several organizations, chief executives have encouraged field-level employees to transmit observations of significance to them at any time. The convenience of e-mail allows the executive to easily forward these observations with his or her comments to the appropriate departments and to request additional information as required. Field sales input, of course, needs to be clear, concise and accurate, but the benefits and ease of use and timely response of this technology give it great potential.

Product Quality Affects More Than Customers

Business must also offer the market products that the sales group is proud to represent and that they are confident will please the customer and fully meet their expectations. Shame is created when a sales force knows that deficiencies will be discovered in their products once put in use. This situation, sometimes forced upon sales organizations, not only demoralizes them but causes customers to regard the company and its salespeople with suspicion in the future.

The mature and trusting relationship that will make a vendor the customer's traditional product source in the future will not be built on deception. The value for a vendor in the Quality Era is in the relationship. The old maxim, "Let the buyer beware," may well have changed to "Let the seller beware." The vendor or salesperson whose product does not deliver what is expected will not get another chance.

During the 1980s, the media ads by American auto manufacturers were claiming achievements in quality that were not always present in their products. But of course a customer might not know this until after the sale, right? Wrong! Millions of business people rented cars when out of town on business and thus had the ability to see and drive a great variety of these vehicles after they had been used for a few thousand miles. The experience was often quite revealing. Automakers may not be fully aware that millions of real-life test drives of their products take place each year through car rentals.

The net result of these "testing" experiences via rental was the opinion that the quality of American automobiles often still had some way to go. What vendors must understand is that trust is destroyed when a product is clearly not up to the claims made for it. They must realize that hype can be discovered in myriad ways they cannot control.

Expanding the Meaning of Value

The concept of value has reached a point from which only the empathetic may proceed. This is a new, evolutionary step that earlier applied only to fashion items. Today, product quality and the proper ambiance surrounding it must be empathetically approached for all products. There is no practical limit to the extent to which the customer value concept can be carried. The concepts of engagement and retention are leading to business linking concepts in which even the vendor/customer interface becomes blurred. New expansions of customer understanding can produce new dimensions of opportunity. Customers who say they want to buy a mousetrap may really be saying that they are in the market for comprehensive pest control. Quality Era salespeople must be able to perceive broad opportunities and to react creatively.

One North Carolina industrial supply business has established a unique supply system for its customers. They sell machine tool bits and work heads to manufacturers in their area. As tool bits are released from the customer's tool bins to their work floor, this information is relayed via a computer link to the supply company, which has assumed the responsibility of maintaining a standard level of each tool bit inventory at each customer location. The resupply is automatic.

The company had found that it cost a customer $75 to issue and track a purchase order; the new system requires no customer purchase orders. The customer's bank account is also automatically debited for payment of each order shipped, thereby eliminating accounts-payable checks (and slow payments).

Since tool bits are issued to specific customer machines and have a projected usage life, the number of tool bits issued can be correlated to the use of a specific customer machine tool to develop a useful preventive maintenance schedule for customer machines. The supply company sends these preventive maintenance reports to each customer every month.

This in-depth customer service ties the customer to the vendor in a most beneficial relationship. Customers receive monthly purchase reports and rebates for quantity purchases credited to their accounts. The preventive maintenance reports would of course be erroneous if any bits were supplied by another vendor. Competition would find it most difficult to improve on this service-based relationship. The supply company also knows on a year-to-date basis what each customer has bought in total business and produced in total profit, and what bits are being used in order to plan inventories and their supply orders.

This concept of partnership, or the bonding of customer to vendor by a superior service structure, can produce a relationship almost impenetrable by ordinary competitors; it is clearly a wave of the future. Quality Era selling calls for value increase through creativity. The challenge is to be partnered in and not to be partnered out. Vendors of differing products and services are also forming partnership arrangements to provide more competitive and comprehensive customer service. Already, many mail-order suppliers have contracted at special delivery rates with overnight delivery services to offer their customers next-day delivery at a modest increase over normal parcel post rates. This, of course, increases the appeal of mail-order shopping and added incremental business for the delivery service.

FedEx of Memphis, Tennessee, well known in the overnight delivery service business, is offering warehouse space and order acceptance service to vendors under a subsidiary, FedEx Logistics Services. Under this system, orders for the vendor's items are received, picked, packed, and shipped by FedEx as part of a service package. The customers get next-day delivery and FedEx gets more business through this partnership with vendors who benefit from rapid delivery.

There has never been a greater selection of resources available to those with the creative capability to use them. The future will belong to the businesses that are creative and empathetic. Quality Era salespeople must use executive-level insight and broader vision to develop and sell these partnership structures.

The sales group must remove their blinders; they must *see* and *hear* with empathetic understanding. What is the customer's real problem? What is the ultimate creative system approach worth to him or her? Quality Era customers are open to the intelligent selling of creative and comprehensive solutions, not just products.

Quality Era salespeople must expand their mission to one of *partnership facilitation* through consultant-level observation. In ancient China, modest ladies of the upper class were reticent to allow themselves to be examined by physicians. So instead of undergoing a genuine physical exam, they sent their servants to the physician with a carved ivory figure of themselves on which the servant was to point out the area that hurt or was involved in a malady. From this the physician was to diagnose and treat the problem. Salespeople who sit and discuss a customer problem when the opportunity to *go and see* is at hand put themselves in the same situation as the Chinese physician. It is foolish to make judgments based on imagination. When possible, go and see.

To gain precise understanding of customer concerns, a new concept called San Gen Shugi is being instituted in Japan. This concept emphasizes an evaluation of the customer's situation based on *actual time*, *actual place*, and *actual product*. When judged appropriate, a team is assembled by the salesperson to go to the customer's location and see and understand the problem in the actual environment in which it occurs. Then and only then is a solution formulated by the team to address the problem.

The partnership examples discussed previously require ongoing personal sales contact to create and maintain. They require ongoing relationships at peer levels within the executive management ranks of the partnership companies. In recent times, a personal sales group has been considered as part of a larger overall strategic and operational group called *marketing*. Businesses are not respectful of tradition in retaining expensive operations when less costly and more effective alternatives are available. If methodologies other than personal selling can cause sufficient numbers of customers to buy, they will be adopted.

Media advertising following a proven strategy designed through market survey research and validated with customer reaction can certainly sell products. Can selling – the marketing of products, the ability to modify a perception of product value with customers – be fully automated and performed remotely? Can other product design methodologies be so perfected and refined toward meeting each customer's perceived needs that the requirement for interpersonal interaction with a salesperson is eliminated? The global market is demonstrating that when the quality level is sufficiently obvious, the price sufficiently low, and there is market visibility, a demand for some products will be created. Japanese cameras are an example of this; they also prove that apparent value can sell a product in spite of its foreign origin. These cameras are, of course, now sold in great volumes via mail order. Possibly money invested in product quality can be considered as money spent on marketing – the product being designed so as to convey much of its own sales message through clearly apparent value.

Selling, Marketing, or Something New

We enter here a question of semantics that must be dealt with, for the traditional sense of the terms "selling" and "sales" may not convey the proper meanings for Quality Era discussion. The term "selling" has traditionally meant "to persuade people to buy," and the group that did the persuading was called "Sales." As other forms of product promotion have been developed, the entire concept, including everything that creates and fulfills customer demand, came to be called "marketing" by some. Many personal salespeople began to call themselves "marketing representatives." This title is possibly appropriate when salespeople command a range of resources directed by their judgment and creativity. Just where sales leaves off and marketing begins is difficult to distinguish. Though this has become more an issue of intrabusiness and academic turfsmanship than an area of customer concern, it profoundly affects attitudes toward selling as a profession. Buried within the semantics are tones of meaning which dissuade and discourage by placing "*sales*" in a less ethical light than "marketing." One very prominent marketing text suggests the following distinction between marketing and selling.

The marketing concept, . . . holds that the key to achieving organizational goals consists in determining the needs and wants of the target markets and delivering the desired satisfaction more effectively and efficiently than competitors. . . . Selling focuses on the needs of the seller; marketing on the needs of the buyer . . . Selling is preoccupied with the seller's need to convert his product into cash; marketing with the idea of satisfying the needs of the customer by means of the product and the whole cluster of things associated with creating, delivering and finally consuming it. . . . Selling is therefore not even the most important part of marketing. Peter Drucker put it this way: There will always, one can assume, be need for some selling. But the aim of marketing is to make selling super-fluous. The aim of marketing is to know and understand the customer so well that the product or service fits him and sells itself. Ideally, marketing should result in a customer who is ready to buy. All that is needed then is to make the product or service available.[1]

This is amazing; the best salespeople and sales organizations have really been "marketing" all along. Making personal selling superfluous is something the accountants would like. It would save a great deal of money that is now spent on a personal sales force. Eliminating selling also appeals to theorists who dislike subjective aspects of a function and desire to reduce behavior to a mathematical certainty.

Is detached "marketing" really capable of the leadership and innovation that captures new markets? Possibly not. As the distance from the customer increases, a status-quo approach can result that merely *reacts* to competition and market data at the level of present consumer attitudes. Who "sells" the customers on new perspectives to take when they consider products? There are many such perspectives possible. In many situations control of the terrain (i.e., the customer's mental perspective) means control of the sales outcome. Value derives from perspective, which can be modified by a logical selling discussion. Sales then follow based on that perspective. Marketing may work in selling purely commodity items, but a conversational interaction capable of altering perspective will often be required for new and innovative products and concepts.

The customer's mind is changing continually. The term "marketing" can imply detachment, a "behind the lines" strategy, great in theory but lacking the personalization that wins the real competitive battles of the Quality Era. Empathetic information flows minute by minute from close, daily customer contact – hearing, seeing, and feeling the customer's perspective of the situation. This is where salespeople are.

Customers who initially are not open to considering a particular product may be resistant due to an incomplete or inaccurate perspective. By suggesting a broader perspective, salespeople can sell a product obliquely. An initial impression of value is formed by each customer for every product when he or she first considers it. This impression could be called the product's "original customer value perception." If the customer's original value perception is left unchallenged, the essential value of personal selling is forfeited, along with a possible sale.

It has been said that selling really begins when a customer states an objection. Customers object when they perceive that the price is too high or the product is inappropriate, but that is often based on an erroneous initial perspective. The leadership and consultant credibility so essential to establishing respect and partnership with the customer is actually earned and sales are made when erroneous preconceptions are corrected. (This essential concept is discussed in more detail in Chapter 5.) Customers, in essence, must "buy into" a new value perspective from which the product is seen to in fact offer a usefulness worth its price. It is this ability of salespeople to establish interactively and empathetically new value perspectives with customers and then use these new attitudes to sell the product that gives salespeople their value. The previous reference to marketing making selling superfluous by so clearly planning to meet customer demand that no "selling" is necessary is possibly more for academic contemplation than actual implementation. This was historically a beautiful theory but, as Mr. Yeltsin and many of his countrymen may attest, not successful in producing products which delighted customers.

Barriers of departmentalization between sales and marketing departments can cause resentment between them and cause them to disconnect from each other. I recently heard of a Fortune 500 company whose sales people were asked to escort marketing survey employees to customer locations in order for customer survey data to be gathered on site. The salespeople were incredulous. They could have easily asked these questions during normal sales visits and, in many cases, felt they already understood customer attitudes toward the products in question. They resented their company wasting money and their time to have this outside group do what they easily could have done and in effect were already doing.

Upper management expects the sales group to move product, but they frequently do not understand that in doing so the sales organization is already applying creativity and customization at every turn, often to overcome problems inherent in the existing marketing plan, which headquarters believes is working as planned. Just because a product is actually selling does not mean that it is selling for the reasons or by the methods anticipated in the original marketing strategy.

Professional salespeople can sell an individualized general or functional perspective first and then sell the product based on it. Thus selling is often a two-step process: selling a solution concept and then selling the product as the specific answer to the conceptual requirement. Attempts to eliminate personal professional sales may be an attempt to oversystematize an inherently unstable system. Variables that cannot be anticipated, reacted to, or analyzed accurately from a distance can cause marketing performance estimates to be only approximately correct at best. Perhaps the term "selling" must be changed and its functions broadened. The Quality Era will demand interactive personal discussion of the value perspective and need concept to help individual customers decide to buy products. In this book, we will call the group that performs this interactive personal communication function the sales group and the individuals who perform this function salespeople. In the future, we may well call them architects of customer value or customer value advocates.

Summary

Beneath the complexity of the new global marketplace lies unparalleled opportunities for businesses with the strategy, vision, and synergy to grasp it. The strategy must be one of differentiation through product quality, product support, and the atmosphere conveyed to customers. A vision of success through teamwork and service to customers must pervade the business through leadership and initiative, not just through reactive management. Empathy must be added to statistics to yield more comprehensive knowledge of customer concerns and their potential solutions. The sales group must take a broader vision of customer problems, potential solutions, and their role in developing their company's success. Management must enable and cultivate a synergy of information technology, motivated employees, quality products, and committed concern for customer delight. Through such synergy the business becomes more than the sum of its parts – it becomes a Quality Era competitor.

References

[1] Kotler, Philip, 1991. *Marketing Management.* New York: Prentice-Hall, p. 16.

CHAPTER 3

PERSONAL PROFESSIONAL SELLING IN THE QUALITY ERA

In the past, salespeople played a more limited role. Historically, the objective of most sales activity could be typified as an incidental encounter that resulted in a conquest called a "sale." Today, the concept is better described as an engagement marked by helpful discussion that leads to an ongoing meeting of minds and a broadening of a sales relationship into a partnership. Rather than work toward an incident that produces a sale, salespeople must engage customers in the development of a relationship that persists and grows with repeated follow-on sales that broaden the range of products sold and deepens the dependence of each on the other. Sales should be made in anticipation that the vendor company will secure a customer who will generate dependable business flow, and that the customer will establish a traditional source point that can be relied upon consistently for an increasing range of products and services.

The importance of engagement by both vendor and customer cannot be underestimated, for as the noise level discussed earlier mounts there is a potential for customers to feel misunderstood and unappreciated, and this causes disengagement due to stress. There are certain items that must be bought and others that can be bought if the customer feels the circumstances are favorable. Customers will make more purchases when they are understood, appreciated, and comfortable with the vendor and salesperson. This might be called an "engaging situation." Customers, remember, are at least as interested in a satisfactory outcome as the vendor.

This touches on a very important philosophical concept that applies to the buying and selling process. There is great security and comfort in being able to rely on custom, tradition, or culture to carry us through stressful situations. We hold traditional weddings, funerals, worship services, and so forth precisely because at particularly stressful times a standard methodology provided by tradition facilitates getting the thing done reliably and properly. Proven guidelines for stressful events are the very reason we have evolved "traditional" methodologies. As Michaly Csikszentmihalyi has pointed out, "Cultures (traditions) are defensive constructions against chaos, designed to reduce the impact of randomness on experience. . . . In doing this we limit possibilities but we derive the ability to channel attention to a more limited set of goals and this allows a more effortless action . . ."[1] This says that humans faced with apparent chaos will seek to gain personal freedom by limiting the things to which they must pay conscious attention. The option of a warm and friendly vendor haven is positive. As the "noise" of the market increases, the tendency to filter selectively will increase. The businesses that enjoy success in the Quality Era will be those that are able to engage customers in a relationship on the customer side of that selective filter and thereby free the customer from the stressful chore of finding sources for a particular product or service.

One marketing consultant of my acquaintance[1] tells an interesting hypothetical story that is rich in this concept:

> One day long ago in the dim past, there was a village where everyone made everything for themselves. Suddenly, one man – I'll call him Aaron – stood up on the stump of a recently cut tree and shouted for everyone to pay attention. The people gathered around to see what he would say; when everything was totally quiet, he said, "I'll make the bread." Now there ensued a great deal of discussion with everyone considering the implications of this. One man said that Aaron could certainly make good bread and it would save time on everyone's part to not have to make bread anymore. Soon, many others suggested that they would become sources of other things and trade with each other and with Aaron for his bread. An economy was thus born.

There was an *implied contract* on Aaron's part that he would, in assuming responsibility for making the bread, make good bread of dependable quality and quantity. Also, the assumption of a particular provisioning function by an individual or business should enable the specialization and improvement of their art through focus and diligence. As Adam Smith outlined, society benefits from this specialization of labor.

Over the last century, the explosive expansion of economies has diverted many Aarons of the business world away from focus on their *implied contract* (to make and deliver a dependable supply of excellent bread). Business management needs to reconsider the responsibility taken up when the sign went over the door reading "insurance," "auto dealer," "furniture," and so forth. Customers still look to any business to fulfill its obligation under this implied contract. Note also that Aaron was at once the production department and the sales group – customer attitudes flowed freely to affect his product because he dealt personally with customers and could modify his product based on direct timely information. This connection can be lost as sales and production are separated when a business expands and the ready flow of information between customers and production is impaired.

The effective sales organization in the Quality Era must be capable of engaging customers and satisfying them completely enough to position the vendor company as the customer's traditional source for the product type now in question and for other products in the future. This is the strategic goal; it is also the status that will be sought and developed by competitors. Businesses that fulfill their implied contract of quality product in dependable supply give sales a valid message to tell. Deming defined quality as the factor that brings customers back again and again and again – to which we might add "for more and more and more."

Slogans such as "Why shop anywhere else?" and "Who could ask for more?" also touch on this concept. If a company's *customers* are in agreement with these phrases, the business is on target. Business organizations that acquire this focus in their marketing strategy and perfect it through their sales groups have the proper vision. Those businesses whose customers do not perceive them in this manner need to focus on engagement strategy. Current sales volumes may be solid and increasing, but an underlying engagement strategy must be at work or ultimately the business will suffer. Nothing masks deficiencies in business like a positive business climate. The sales group takes the heat when business is slow, and they are quite capable of happily accepting praise when business is good. Management needs to view the organization's sales effectiveness objectively, particularly during these times of plenty; this is the safest protection against business downturns, which will certainly come. "Good business times" offer management the opportunity to implement quality-oriented sales processes. This is much easier than reacting to a sudden crisis. In fact, times of good business should be viewed primarily as opportunities for structural improvement.

Deming emphasized that under contemporary management approaches employees are often blamed for poor performance and rewarded for strong performance when the real factors contributing to success and failure were essentially random and outside their control. The Quality Era calls for an honest evaluation and renovation of sales structures, support systems, and sales strategy in businesses that are often, in truth, coasting on circumstance. The sales group should be capable of making things happen, not just watching things happen. Timing is always crucial. Luck can overcome a degree of ineptitude, but the best combination is talent and solid strategy attacking solid opportunity. Many contemporary sales organizations simply hope to be in the right place at the right time and manage to avoid doing the wrong thing. This is not a sufficiently proactive strategy.

A Selling Organization

What is the proper expectation for a personal sales group in the Quality Era? How should they go about engaging customers and securing traditional supplier relationships? Does the vendor organization need a personal professional sales organization at all, or can this engaging and confirming process be accomplished by a more efficient means? These are questions that management must consider.

Personal professional salespeople are of value to a vendor and can be used profitably when marketing a product that can justify *customized personal interaction* with the customer in order to secure his or her business and ongoing commitment. It is an old cliché that if you build a better mousetrap, the world will beat a path to your door. In this new, noisy world, however, there are many mousetraps. Professional salespeople interactively relate the new mousetrap to the particular needs of individual customers. Sales groups can also seek out customers rather than waiting for them to hear about the new trap and come to see the vendor. The salesperson should be able to explain why the new trap is really better when everyone else is saying that their's is the best. The world might eventually beat a path to the vendor's door, but the producer may be dead and gone before benefits can be realized. To ensure that they will be able to enjoy the fruits of their labor within their own lifetime, vendors use salespeople to speed the discovery process. Windows of opportunity are opening and closing with greater rapidity. Even though one vendor's trap is best today, a better one may be introduced by another vendor tomorrow. The United States Patent Office has received applications for over 3,500 mousetrap designs. Only a few have enjoyed market success. When left to be discovered independently by customers, they may not be discovered at all. Only the ones that receive market visibility have a chance of being sold.

A sales group should bring in more than its operating budget. The sales department should generate sufficient business volumes over other potential marketing methodologies to justify its existence and to pay for the trouble of its administration. Typically, companies that market products that are priced relatively high with significant margin fall within this category. Examples might include the insurance, industrial equipment, automobile, home construction, and boatbuilding industries. Through effective, interactive discussion with the potential buyer, sales should produce buying decisions and demonstrate loyalty to the vendor company in a fashion superior to other approaches.

Another important aspect is that the sales group should not lose business for the company by handling customer and prospect opportunities inefficiently. Customers are becoming increasingly sensitive. They resent it when they are not given sufficient attention, when they are misunderstood, or when they are communicated with ineffectively. Customers feel that their time is valuable; they must feel that the time they spend with salespeople is time well spent. Customers enjoy interacting with effective salespeople who are genuinely interested in them and can give competent advice.

Bad Business

A converse concept applies to salespeople: they should not bring in bad business for their company. The truth is that some customers can cost the vendor more than they are worth in terms of slow payment, requirements for unusual services, and even improper use of the product. Salespeople in the Quality Era must focus on consistent quality in presenting their company's product and in the "quality of customers" they bring to the vendor. (Many authors refer to this focus as establishing win/win relationships.) Both parties must benefit from a correctly established relationship in which the vending company supplies products and services that meet or exceed the requirements of the customer, and, in return, the customer complies with their side of the bargain by proper use and payment for the product.

This focus on a more mature approach to customers is not meant to imply that the customer is not, in a sense, "the boss," but that the boss must be reasonable and represent good business for the vendor firm. The goal is for mutual benefit to ensue from the relationship between the company and the customer that the salesperson has established. Customers who do not respond properly to their obligations or who misuse the product or do not service it properly can represent business that is better avoided. Quality Era business will be played on the high plane of a quality product being sold at a relatively high price but representing solid value. There will always be some companies who overstate product quality, and these will appeal to a customer set seeking the lowest price and interested more in a "deal" than in solid value. Vendors and customers who refuse to rise above this level will tend to deal with each other and will risk producing their own recurring set of disasters because their business philosophy is unsound.

Upon being asked by customers for a quality product for a

ridiculously low price, one experienced salesman countered with a question: "Mr. Customer, have you ever contemplated what percent of human misery is the result of someone's getting a deal?" A smile and an understanding nod was the most usual answer. (The discussion then usually moved on to a more fruitful discussion level of quality solutions at *reasonable* prices.) There must be a special hell occupied by "cheap" products bought at "deal" prices. They deserve each other, and Quality Era business strategy does not focus on that market.

John Ruskin sums up the issue of "deal-getting" this way:

> It is unwise to pay too much, but it is worse to pay too little. When you pay too much, you lose a little money – that is all. When you pay too little you sometimes lose everything, because the thing you bought was incapable of doing the thing it was bought to do. The common law of business balance prohibits paying a little and getting a lot – it can't be done. If you deal with the lowest bidder, it is well to add something for the risk you run, and if you do that, you will have enough to pay for something better.[2]

He also emphasizes the risk to customers who seek out low price versus quality in vendors: "There is hardly anything in the world that some man cannot make a little shoddier and sell a little cheaper, and people who consider price only are this man's lawful prey."

Salespeople should be held responsible for the quality of business they generate. The need to institute quality relationships with new customers will necessitate the recruitment of sales personnel who are capable of taking a broader view of business opportunities – who can evaluate opportunities from management's perspective. It takes a measure of selfless insight for salespeople to determine that a situation will not result in an advantage for both the vendor company and customer and then to reject it as bad business. Customers will often need to be educated in a tactful and reasonable fashion as to why the terms of doing business as proposed by the vendor company are in reality the best for all involved. There is an art in helping customers see the logic of a quality approach to business without offending them in the process. The 18th-century philosopher Alexander Pope summed up this subtle art when he said, "Men should be taught as if you taught them not." The tone of the discussion must be logical so that the customer is allowed to discover the validity of the vendor's position. Salespeople must understand the logic of their company's terms and conditions for doing business and be able to confidently explain the "quality rationale" of these to customers. Solid engagement leading to partnership is built on each party's understanding of the other's business perspective.

The most common aspect of deal-making that can compromise the vendor company is pressure from a customer to cut price. Sometimes pricing flexibility is possible, but always within bounds that retain profitability for the vendor company. Customers must understand that if a vendor does not make a profit it will not stay in business and therefore will not be able to give the long-term quality service they themselves will require. It is much to the advantage of a company to have salespeople capable of explaining why a product is worth its stated price in terms of value than to have them attempting to "buy" sales by discounting price.

The Essential Value of Personal Selling

Products should be worth the price requested, and professional salespeople must be capable of explaining why the price is fair – or even low – as set. This is precisely the point of value of the salesperson, that *he or she is able to leverage the perception of value in the eyes of the customer* so that it is perceived to be well above the asking price. This talent for empathetic personal interaction with customers so that the product's value is communicated directly to them in their own terms is the essential value of personal sales contact.

The value of a salesperson is tied directly to his or her ability to perform this function. When a product's price is discounted by a salesperson, what is conceded to the customer is margin often equating to pure profit. The product will still have to be manufactured and delivered and the vendor company will still have to provide support and handle the administrative details. Thus what is given up when price is discounted is the most important component to the vendor company: its profit. Given an effective selling process (such as the one outlined in Chapter 5), salespeople, who do not or cannot explain why the price requested by the vendor for their product is reasonable in light of the benefits that will accrue to customers, are representing the wrong product or the wrong company or may even be in the wrong profession. This is the very essence of the sales function.

Effective Quality Era selling will require sales personnel who understand the value structure of their company's products. Value can be presented from many different perspectives for each product and to each customer. The challenge for the professional salesperson is to present the most appealing yet valid perspective from which a product can be viewed by a particular customer. A product can be evaluated from many different facets or "value perspectives," as suggested by Fig. 3.1. For each customer or prospect – and for each product – there is a perspective from which the maximum value is perceived, from which the maximum benefit to the customer is seen and the cost, therefore, made most acceptable. Discovering and presenting this perspective is the essence of selling. The salesperson must empathetically understand the value concepts these perspectives represent and which apply to each customer and product.

The conquest-type selling of earlier times implied a customer who was left with the product and a salesperson who has left with the money. The implication from this scenario is that there can be regret on the part of the customer when the excitement of the sales pitch is gone and he or she is left with the product and no longer has the money. The type of relationship we seek to build in the Quality Era requires that sales will be made so that the customer will appreciate the product's value at the time of the sale, on the day following the sale, and on into the future, and that he or she will appreciate and respect the salesperson and the vendor company for providing them with

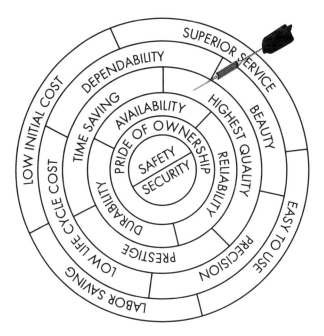

Figure 3.1. Levels of value perspective.

honest value. Quality, remember, is what keeps customers coming back again and again [Deming].

An old term for the disillusionment that can set in following a sale was "buyer's remorse," and its avoidance was probably was the basis for the old Latin adage, "caveat emptor" – "let the buyer beware." Even in Roman times the customer was to be careful in sales situations because there was a danger of not getting what was really expected after parting with real money! The salespeople of the Quality Era must guard both against buyers being disillusioned and the vendor being exploited. In fact, if they are to produce a delighted customer, salespeople will need to fit a product so well to a customer, and at such a price, that the product is in fact undersold. Customers will then find that they got even more than they thought they were buying and that the vendor and the salesperson anticipated their needs better than they did themselves.

As customers, we know that it is a pleasing thing to find a product to be even better in use than anticipated when it was bought – to find after some time in use that the price paid was not only reasonable but that, if we had understood at the time of purchase how good, or effective, or enjoyable it would be in use, we might have paid even more. When we have enjoyed this feeling about a product, we are a delighted customer and the salesperson who "sold" it did us a service. This is the type of sale for which the salespeople of the Quality Era must strive. It is this type of sale that builds enjoyment and appreciation in customers and enthusiasm for products and the company that makes and sells them. The sale is solid, benefiting everyone involved, and the customer is delighted and tells others. Delighted customers become an adjunctive sales force, and the sales group of such a business finds pride in their company and joy in their work.

John Ruskin, remember, contended that "personal wealth consists in the possession of many items that are useful." This thought implies that if a thing is owned but not of use it is of little or no benefit to its owner. This concept reminds us that the enjoyment or value that a customer will realize from a product is directly related to his or her ability to make use of it. This means that customer education and product knowledge can tangibly increase a product's value by increasing its usefulness. Quality Era selling will involve suiting products to the customer and suiting customers for the product. Value can therefore be tangibly increased through product support. This requires an empathetic understanding of the customer and what they need to fully utilize the product.

Today many companies are finding that if the customer is educated in the proper care and use of a product, satisfaction is, in fact, greatly increased; the opportunity to create a delighted customer is enhanced. Such supplemental education can take the form of clearly written and illustrated directions for proper product use. Using Quality Era technology, it can also take the form of recorded audio-cassette tape, or even video tape, demonstrating all facets of product use and service. For new products vendors should always perform an empathetic "walk through" as if they were a customer opening the box and putting the product to use for the first time. Whenever this walk through uncovers a question or assembly issue or anything unclear, this should be remedied so that the customer will not encounter the same difficulty. It is this kind of caring that builds delighted customers.

Henckels, the German maker of kitchen cutlery, recently began selling a 20-minute video tape with one of its famous kitchen knives as an introductory package. This is a powerful sales approach designed to ensure that customers understand the use and care of fine kitchen cutlery. This video demonstration features a noted chef showing how to cut everything from common vegetables to ornate decorative items. There is much to learn about the proper use and care of cutlery that the new consumer may not know. Of course the demonstrations featured require a "sharp" knife and one of the proper style and balance, which draws a contrast for the customer between the new Henckels knife and the older, less well-designed knives in the average kitchen. As customers try this new knife according to these video instructions, they should come to understand why knives of this design are worth their premium price. This added level of new customer education in a design concept is powerful because it contains a concept called *imprinting*. This concept has great applicability in Quality Era selling.

Imprinting

Imprinting is the term used by students of animal behavior that applies to the tendency of the young of a species to mentally and emotionally fixate on something soon after its birth. An example of this is the fact that a newly hatched duckling will identify the first thing it sees move – even a block of wood pulled by a string – as its mother and will follow it everywhere. This is not a concept unique to the animal kingdom; maternal bonding is encouraged at the birth of a human infant when it is brought in close contact with its mother so that a firm, reinforced, dependent identity is formed. The reason in nature for imprinting is that it is important to survival.

Though certainly not as intense as infant imprinting but still important is the imprinting that can take place when a vendor company "opens our eyes" to an innovative design concept that enhances the usefulness and potential enjoyment of its product. From that point on, customers tend to inspect all products for similar design principles and judge them deficient when the concept is not present. Whether it is "no more tears" from a shampoo, a "throwaway bag" from an Electrolux vacuum cleaner, or other more subtle design features, the imprinting of such features is important in product identity and in establishing customer loyalty. Perhaps Henckels could not justify the production of a video tape on kitchen cutlery to sell one knife. However, Henckels is not selling just one knife; it is selling the Henckels concept of cutlery, a standard against which others will be measured. As time goes by, that first knife will grow to a collection, and the user will be using and caring for them with a new knowledge and respect. Henckels may become the automatic and traditional source supplier for additional kitchen knives for more and more customers.

Of course, as Henckels knives find favor and allegiance from customers, there is an implication that since one type of product bearing the name or trademark of the company is of trusted quality, other items produced by the company will incorporate the same levels of design quality and customer understanding. Thus, Henckels is enjoying brisk sales and high customer expectations for its kitchen towels, knife sharpeners, scissors, and knife storage blocks. The concept here is to differentiate oneself through one product and then enjoy the status of having passed inside the customer's noise filter to become an imprinted, "traditional," and desired source supplier for a certain class of items; in this case, not just kitchen cutlery but related items bearing a now-trusted label. A company can establish and implement a comprehensive selling strategy for one product that will benefit all its merchandise simultaneously.

We can find, however, that even when carefully planned strategy is implemented, a product can take on a dynamic after its introduction that was unforeseen during its marketing strategy development phase. It is imperative that these new twists that occur in the actual marketplace be understood immediately and communicated to the vendor company so that if the dynamic is resulting in a problem it can be corrected before negative imprinting can occur. Conversely, if the dynamic has positive implications, it can be immediately reinforced to maximize opportunity. The organization in most constant and intimate contact with the market and the customer is the sales group. The Quality Era sales force must be used effectively to relate the facts back to management for appropriate action. Strategy is only strategy. In the marketplace, reality rapidly replaces strategy. Unforeseen variables and issues can become factors in customer decision factors. If companies are to prosper, market realities must rapidly penetrate to vendor management so that strategies can be modified. Quality Era businesses must expect and plan for rapid reaction to market reality. Excessive rigidity of strategy can make a company appear foolish to customers and result in wasted opportunities. Strategy must be given a chance, but reality must predominate. There is something ludicrous about a ship's captain maintaining that his vessel is designed to be "unsinkable" while he is standing knee-deep in rising seawater.

In April of 1985, the Coca-Cola Company converted to a new formulation of Coca-Cola that had, supposedly, more modern taste so that it could compete more effectively with Pepsi and other colas making inroads into its sales. Marketing research and testing had indicated that customers would like the new formulation. Coca-Cola announced that it would change the formula and then replaced the old product with the new one.

Customers in the real world did not react as anticipated. They had come to expect a specific taste when they opened a can or bottle of Coca-Cola. The imprinting and expectation of a distinct flavor had been built over many years, and customers protested and rejected the new product. With remarkable agility, Coca-Cola realized that it was up against a powerful dynamic of customer expectation, so they relabeled the old formula and made it again available as "Classic Coke." Though the formula switches, relabeling, and renaming were expensive, the results in terms of publicity and customer desire for the old product restored their declining sales. Some competitors even suggested that Coca-Cola had never been genuinely committed to a product change but had intended only to draw publicity and renewed attention to its traditional product.

This is perhaps a case of an "accident" having a better outcome than a strategy – even a strategy developed by one of the world's largest and best corporations with enormous resources dedicated to customer research and product development. There was a dynamic at work in the consumer world that was not understood at corporate headquarters. Coca-Cola, in its "classic" form, had become one of those dependable "safe harbor" products in the sea of chaos. Customers did not want to be set adrift in regard to cola selection; their allegiance was to a product, not to the Coca-Cola Company. Coca-Cola found that its original formula was one of the anchor points of a society. It was as American as baseball and apple pie. Coca-Cola had attempted not just to change a drink but to violate a tradition, to tamper with imprinted reality. Customers felt that they owned the classic Coca-Cola recipe and openly resented the fact that the company would be so unfeeling as to change it. Coca-Cola had sufficient good sense and was in tune enough with its marketplace that it was able to modify and remedy this failing strategy, though they may have temporarily lost some luster in the eyes of the public.

I recently heard a presentation by an executive of one of America's leading household product manufacturers, who stated with a great deal of pride that after years of work with models and consumer surveys, his company was able to predict with about 80-percent accuracy what the market reaction would be to a product such as frozen orange juice. There are many more complex products than orange juice, which is almost a commodity-level product. The possibility that a new marketing strategy may miss the mark is still fairly high. The company that will succeed in the Quality Era will be the one that is prepared to modify and change its strategy and is structured to obtain timely information that will indicate when its strategy is in error.

Another example of a product market dynamic that lies outside company strategy is Straight Arrow Products, Inc. of

Phillipsburg, New Jersey. Straight Arrow is a small company that manufactures and distributes products for the equestrian market – that is, for horses. One of its products, "The Hoofmaker," is, according to the label, "an intensive protein hoof treatment" that is mixed with water and applied to the horse's hooves by hand to strengthen the hooves and keep them in fine show-horse condition. Apparently, horsewomen who applied this formulation to their horse's hooves discovered that their own fingernails stopped splitting and attained a new and healthier look. They told their friends, and it is now almost impossible for the drugstores in our city to keep "The Hoofmaker" cream in stock because college coeds are buying it up as fast as it arrives on the shelf. In addition, Straight Arrow also makes "Mane 'N Tail and Body" shampoo for horses, which is also enjoying great success with these same humans. Nowhere on the label is there any indication that this product is intended for any other than veterinary use. A new dynamic has taken over with this product, and the new customer-discovered use for it could propel this small company into the cosmetic stratosphere.[2]

This concept of discovering what is really happening at the customer level is analogous to the importance on the battlefield of being aware of what is happening at the front lines. The most effective military commanders in history were those who focused on knowing the real situation in a timely fashion and modified their strategy to take advantage of opportunities or to counter adverse conditions. History is replete with accounts of military commanders who, far from the action, thought that their strategy was working when in fact the military situation had developed in unexpected ways from the opening shot of the battle. Accurate, firsthand, front-line information on almost a minute-by-minute basis is a function that the sales group can and should provide if they are properly organized and trained as observers and reporters on the customers' attitudes and their reactions to products.

Another example may illustrate how easy it is for a business to snatch defeat from the jaws of victory. One of the oldest slogans within one of America's foremost computer companies was "Sell education – education sells." This referred to the concept that the better customers understood how to use a computer, the better able they were to obtain the results they expected and thereby become satisfied customers. Conducting training classes for customers also generated some revenue for the company, though not anything to compare with that produced by computer hardware and software sales.

A much more profound dynamic was at work in this vendor's offerings of low-cost computer courses in almost every major city. Customers who were considering a computer purchase attended these courses after being invited by vendor sales personnel. Upon finding the computers offered by this manufacturer to be user friendly, they became more enthusiastic about their ability to manage and use computers in their business after their hands-on experience in class.

The classes were taught by the vendor's systems engineering personnel, who were the same people who would be assigned to assist in the customer installation of the newly purchased equipment. As instructors, these engineers gained the confidence and respect of the potential customers who attended their classes. Personnel from companies considering purchasing computer equipment were attending classes with representatives from other businesses that had already ordered – and in some cases had already installed – the vendor's equipment. Thus, an atmosphere of security and camaraderie was developed in new, prospective customers who saw the friendly resources available for their support, the quality of personnel who would support their installation, and the numerous other businesses similar to theirs that were progressing satisfactorily with installation of computer equipment.

Discussion among customer personnel during coffee and lunch breaks at these classes often involved revelations of higher pay levels and career advancement for those who were taking responsibility for installing and operating the new computer systems. The net result was a vision that vendor support was strong, that learning the vendor's computer operation could further one's career and earnings potential, and that a new and comforting group of friends in neighboring businesses were proceeding on their projects together. This powerful marketing advantage was fully understood and utilized by field sales personnel to capture and maintain market leadership.

The dynamic produced by these classes was not so well understood by the management team at the vendor company's headquarters. In an efficiency review of all field departments, it was found that *education* was not paying its way as a "profit center." It was redesigned and *"improved"* with a new automated approach that used computer-assisted instruction. Under this new approach, a student was essentially left alone with a personal computer and made responsible to schedule his or her own educational time. The new approach eliminated the powerful classroom dynamic that was making a profound contribution to sales success. The older education format had imprinted a new standard of expectation for education that other vendors did not meet, often eliminating them from consideration through a perceived deficiency.

Management needs to understand what is really selling their products. Products often are not selling for the assumed or obvious reasons or through the assumed and obvious sales techniques. The dynamic often lies deeper.

The Quality Era will be dominated by the company that is empathetic – that is in touch with the customers' attitudes and feelings. Business management must react rapidly as situations change to build and retain its traditional supplier status with its current customers and to grow its customer base. The successful business will know its market identity and its products and how both are being perceived by its customers. This business will be enhanced and will build on its strengths. It will be aware of and put in place innovations that secure its strengths and correct its weaknesses. It will, above all, receive its primary motivation from delighting customers and enjoying the business benefits that flow from the customer relationships that they continuously confirm and develop. Their policies will make sense at the ground level. Their management will look to their sales groups to be their eyes and ears in the area of empathetic understanding of the customer. The ability to function in this manner must be facilitated by top management, and the sales force must, if necessary, be trained in a broader role with more effective use of new internal channels of communication. The focus of the future is to engage, retain, and cultivate customers.

Summary

The Quality Era will require a broader, dual role for professional salespeople. They must engage, sell, and retain customers for the business as well as actively interpret market dynamics and customer attitudes and needs to their management. They will become, in effect, the switchboard operators of the business to customers and, just as importantly, the customer-to-business communications link. In doing this, they must become more adept in understanding their customers and in perceiving value. The salespeoples' value to a business lie in their ability to interactively leverage or change the customer's original perception of product value. In this function, they must be sensible of the outcome for both their customer and their company, for both are in fact their customer.

References

[1] Csikszentmihalyi, Michaly, 1990. *Flow: The Psychology of Optimal Experience.* New York: Harper & Row.

[2] Neave, H. R., 1990. *The Deming Dimension.* Knoxville, TN: SPC Press, p. 310.

Notes

1. Harlan Caruthers, College of Business Administration, University of Tennessee.

2. I tried unsuccessfully for a week to contact this company in regard to buying some of its stock, if available, but I could not get anyone to answer the phone. They are possibly too busy with their unanticipated success.

CHAPTER 4

THE SALES PERSONALITY

The closer one views today's business organizations, the more evident it becomes that various component departments within a business often do not communicate effectively with each other. There are a variety of reasons for this and chief among them is the often disparate measurement criteria used for performance evaluation.[1] These differing measurements are frequently in conflict with the performance criteria used by other departments and are often counterproductive for the organization overall.

For example, an administrative group may be given incentives to keep accounts receivable at the lowest possible level, and yet some flexibility in allowing slower payment might allow the sales group to generate orders from customers who are having temporary difficulty making payments. The sales organization may desire the largest possible inventory from which to deliver so that no item is ever out of stock, and yet if this desire for a 100-percent service level is honored, the investment in inventory can become astronomical. Business management must strive not only to improve communication between departments but also to establish measurement systems encouraging a level of team performance that is in line with the overall objectives of the business.

This chapter will deal with some general and prevailing aspects of the "sales personality" in the hope that, when these attitudes are understood by management and possibly by other departmental personnel, communication based on empathetic understanding can ensue. In dealing with anyone, we can benefit from empathetic understanding of the other person's perspective and personality – what motivates them and how they see their job. Effective communication is always personality to personality. Teamwork is built on personal understanding and professional respect.

Sales

It has been accurately stated that nothing happens in business until someone sells something. In most businesses sales are the sole source of revenue (in) – everything else is expense (out). The sales group makes sales happen. Through a more insightful understanding of the sales group, other departments may be enabled to give members of this important cadre better support in terms of product design, delivery, services, and general marketability. As it becomes better understood by the other departments, the sales organization can more freely contribute to overall business performance. By integrating all departments through sales awareness, a selling organization is produced.

Another important aspect is for management to consider their present sales group in light of the characteristics presented here. Are the right people being hired for sales? Is the training program imparting the right skills? Do sales personnel carry an appropriate attitude toward themselves and toward their profession? Management's goal should be a sales group that will be selling satisfactory business volumes and showing genuine pleasure in the job itself. If these individuals are performing a job they thoroughly enjoy and are proud to perform, financial rewards will follow for everyone.

A Somewhat Lonely Job

Because personal professional selling is ultimately a one-on-one function, it is sometimes a lonely function that is poorly understood by outsiders. As with many jobs performed by professionals, the selling function can appear easy to the casual observer. Movements performed by a professional athlete often appear effortless, but the sports professional is drawing on deep resources of knowledge, training, and habit to make the function appear easy. The same holds true for the effective salesperson. His or her actions will seldom appear strained and never contrived. The function of the salesperson in the Quality Era is to use the art of persuasion at a consultant level to bring about an initial purchase that will satisfy or delight the customer and thus win the customer's respect and long-term loyalty for the vendor firm. This is best performed within an atmosphere of easy, open, and honest conversation. This will often make professional salespeople appear to be performing an easy job that requires only an outgoing personality and a gift for conversational showmanship. That appearance is deceptive. It is the depth of personal resource that directly produces the desired cordial sales atmosphere. It is not accidental.

Perception of the Sales Role

When Arthur Miller wrote *Death of a Salesman*, he portrayed Willie Loman, the salesman, as a bumbling, tired old man who thought he could succeed on "a smile and a shoeshine." Willie came abruptly to the end of his dream as a broken man stripped of his illusions. His customers had stopped smiling back; they had also stopped buying.

Unfortunately, this image of salespeople has been pervasive and powerful. It has wielded a very negative impact on millions of potential salespeople, causing them to choose other careers. It has negatively colored the thinking of whole generations of managers and of the public in general. What Arthur Miller did not say, however, was that not only did Willie Loman die, but the *whole era* of selling that he represented died as well. Gone is that era of isolated, small-town markets where any and all merchandise new from the big city was always of interest. The marketplace has matured; modern professional salespeople bear little resemblance to Willie. Sales today can be one of the most personally fulfilling and financially rewarding professions – for those who pursue it correctly.

It was a perfectly natural reaction to look down on Willie Loman. He had little technical or business competence – and he felt he didn't need it. People bought because they liked Willie Loman, not because they understood or appreciated his product. His motivation for selling was really immediate personal gain. Selling in today's more sophisticated market requires a depth Willie lacked. The sales role today requires a professional salesperson. Willie Loman was not a professional.

Webster defines a profession as "a calling requiring specialized knowledge," and a professional as "one who is characterized by or conforms to the technical standards of a profession." We could add that modern professionals have made a positive commitment to a specific career and have dedicated significant thought and energy to delivering the highest quality performance in that career. A professional will work to improve his or her skills, to become better in the future, and to modify his or her techniques as the environment changes.

The new Quality Era sales professional will focus on using persuasive talents to the long-term benefit of all parties involved. Rather than a selfish focus, the emphasis will be on customer delight with the product.[2] A key maxim to remember: *All customer dissatisfaction comes from unmet expectations*. Each of us has at some time acquired an object that has given us lasting satisfaction; conversely, we have purchased items that were bought with high expectations but that proved disappointing in use. Toward the salesperson who sold us the item that gives us delight we have a feeling of appreciation and respect; toward the one who sold us a nonperforming item our feelings range from a lack of respect for their competence to an actual questioning of their ethics. Management must understand that, as customers, salespeople have experienced these feelings, too, and do not wish to be put in a position of selling a product that will not perform because it forces the salesperson to incur the feelings of distrust or lost respect that are engendered in customers who are disillusioned.

Empathy, as mentioned by Adam Smith, is the modern professional salesperson's most useful tool in developing a sales case for a particular customer. That same keen empathy allows the salesperson to feel the disappointment produced by an inferior product as well as to enjoy the delight produced in the satisfied customer. The desire to empathetically participate in the delight of a customer may be the single most important factor behind the enthusiasm exhibited by salespeople. If they feel that their product will delight their customer, they can view a sales call as doing the prospect a favor rather than an intrusion. Enthusiasm and a positive attitude are essential to energize a salesperson – a lack of these will produce dismal sales results. Seldom does the enthusiasm of a customer exceed the enthusiasm shown by the salesperson. The product must allow the salesperson to be genuinely enthusiastic.

Morality in Selling

The self-image of salespeople as agents who can improve the lives of others by selling their products makes sales a noble profession and is essential to self-respect and confidence.

Some years back, I was given the opportunity to teach a special, concentrated, one-week sales course to computer sales personnel in the Republic of Ireland. I was no further than a half an hour into an initial discussion of sales techniques when I sensed a lack of engagement with my audience, which I found unusual and disturbing. I stopped and asked, "What's the problem? Why aren't we together?" A brief discussion ensued from which we were able to ascertain that some in this audience saw sales and selling as a calling only a shade removed from theft. The idea of intruding on a perfectly happy businessman and making him unhappy with his present accounting system, only to "sell" him something, did not seem exactly moral. "Then why are you doing it at all?" I asked. "One has to make a living," they replied, "and besides, we don't intend to do it always. Perhaps with some degree of sales success or good fortune we can accumulate enough money to buy some land. Land ownership and raising livestock *is* a worthy profession."

In terms of character, hospitality, and conversational excellence, I had never dealt with a finer group. Their innate honesty had allowed this issue to surface so quickly in the first place. But this excellent group of potential salespeople had not met their sales objective in five years. There was a need to deal with the morality of selling before considering anything else. The very sensitivity to right and wrong and to appropriate behavior that this group exhibited made them ideal candidates for sales, but this same sensitivity stood in their way. Since then, I have usually begun discussions of selling with a clarification of why the profession, pursued properly, is highly ethical and a major contributor to the historical betterment of human life.

With this sales group, we discussed the realistic need for better business information. I related the personal testimony of specific customers who used computer systems and the beneficial impact of this technology – not only on their businesses and profits but also on management, who for the first time felt they could make sense of their business situation, and on clerical workers, who found themselves going home at decent hours to their families rather than working overtime dealing with manually derived information that was never really correct.

This group lacked the sure confidence that the products of their company would truly improve the customers' lives. If salespeople have products they believe in, and which they know will make a positive impact on the quality of life of their customer, they can pursue their work with more complete enthusiasm. But if they lack that certainty, the resulting compromised focus and energy can be the "little difference that makes all the difference" in sales performance. That is why companies in this age of unparalleled competition and emphasis on quality must give their salespeople products, services, and customer support their salespeople will be proud to recommend to customers. It is the salesperson who must face the customer and place his or her personal integrity on the line in recommending a product. It is he or she who has not performed if the recommended product does not meet expectations. This sales group made their sales objectives for the first time the year of our visit and for several years following. I believe a major reason was a new perspective on the legitimacy of selling a legitimately beneficial product.

Commitment

The damage of the stereotypical Willie Loman image has to be put to death with finality. Unaddressed, it hampers commitment to the job and penalizes performance. The best way to deal with these doubts is exposure to the testimony of satisfied and delighted customers so that their delight is verified firsthand.

Management should plan to place new salespeople in immediate contact with their company's best and most loyal customers. Here customers sell the salespeople. It is surprising how much customers enjoy telling new salespeople about their products and their company. Later, when objections and complaints come about a product or service from other quarters, the memory of these satisfied and delighted customers is defense against depression. It also leads the salesperson to discern why some customers were delighted and others were not. This can teach the salesperson the proper product/customer placement that produces the most likely success pattern for their products.

Commitment is second only to a proper perspective on the morality of selling. Commitment to a product and company can be built, as indicated previously, by positive customer contact and from a genuine enthusiasm for the product. Some salespeople must honestly determine whether they can "commit" to selling the world's finest zippers or if they would really rather sell automobiles. This decision is not as simple as it might appear, for there is great variety in zippers and in their use, which, when understood, can yield creative challenge equal to that of selling any other item. The world would be worse off without zippers and even more worse off with zippers that don't work. Who will spread the word? Zipper salespeople, that's who.

Evangelistic Spirit

Salespeople are the Paul Reveres of the free-enterprise system. The best of them will always want to get the word out. It helps to have a personality that tends to want to spread good news to any who will listen. The image of a stand-up showman is not essential, but salespeople do need the ability to initiate and carry on a genuinely enthusiastic conversation that will maintain the interest of the customer. You can't very well make progress by presenting your card and sitting there looking at your customer. Selling is proactive engagement. Salespeople must make sales happen; this would not occur without their presence. They speed up buying decisions; business would move much more slowly without them. They are a catalyst to the chemistry of buying.

Since salespeople help things along, they require a degree of initiative when speaking with customers. Numerous texts are available on sales technique that enumerate various methods for structuring sales calls and insuring customer interaction. These suggest very useful approaches that can be used with benefit by almost any salesperson. Although techniques are useful, they must be underpinned by proper concept and perspective. It is in the areas of concept and perspective that most of the fundamental gaps and deficiencies in modern sales presentations lie.

Determination and Desire for Success

Some years ago, I was given the unique opportunity to help develop a new business sales school for IBM in Atlanta, Georgia. The focus of this program was to train new IBM personnel in the selling of midsize business computer systems.

Possibly the greatest personal benefit from this experience was my daily contact with the staff of this school, which was selected from the company's top salespeople from across the United States. I welcomed the opportunities for discussion so I could determine which techniques had made them effective. After months of discussion and observation, I came to an unexpected conclusion: The personal sales techniques were as numerous and varied as the members of the staff. The common thread was commitment. It was as if the force of determination and enthusiasm that was common to these talented people seemed to find its way out of each individual in the form of techniques that were appropriate to that particular personality. Some used charts and graphs, and some used well-written letters. Some prospected by phone, and others could not believe that salespeople could effectively prospect using anything other than mail or face-to-face visits.

This discovery has strong implications for sales training because one can conclude that new salespeople need to be exposed to a wide variety of techniques in order to allow the selection of those that best fit their personality. The energy to perfect these personal skills has to come from a commitment and determination to succeed. It takes a "fire" within an individual to allow the polishing and buffing of the real marketplace to do its work and make techniques performed originally out of training become habit and an integral part of the individual sales personality. Soldiers have a term to describe those who have been under fire that hints at the change in attitude that forever separates them from those who have not: "the honorable fraternity of those who have been shot at." A somewhat similar situation exists among salespeople who in facing customers have discovered their own unique sales personality. If salespeople seem a little "cocky" within a business organization, it is because they see themselves as the fighter pilots on the business aircraft carrier. They have discovered that, under the stress of competition, they have developed the personal, persuasive force to sell.

General structural techniques learned in sales training will carry an individual through in making sales calls until that salesperson establishes his or her own personal talents. If certain methods are not working, a review of them and the selection of others is in order. Overall concepts presented in training guide the new salesperson in structuring sales presentations and give them a framework on which their individualized professional sales personality will be overlaid.

Conversational Competence

The best salespeople are guided by empathy. They are sensitive to the feelings of customers that accompany the specific needs they voice. Conversationally, the effective salesperson is adept in conveying a feeling of understanding and interest in the customer's "problem," which is seen and felt from the customer's point of view. It has been said that possibly the greatest human emotional need is to feel understood by another individual. In fact, one theory of selling suggests that customers often buy more because they feel that the salesperson understands their needs and feelings, and not because the customer really understands the product. The ability to listen with sincere understanding to the customer and convey that feeling to him or her is of paramount importance in selling. The listening must be nonjudgmental, accepting, and helpful. The air of an engaging and enlightening discussion should be created. Effective sales-people must be able to carry on an interesting conversation, moving toward a perceived logical solution of the customer's problem.

Since people can only carry a limited number of details in their minds at any given time, it is best to approach a sales call with the genuine enthusiasm of a detective who is on a case to help a client find an answer to a problem. A sincere desire to help and be of service is never out of place; when selling is approached from that perspective, the rest will take care of itself. In-depth product knowledge (that is, knowing where your product has been – or could be – used to real advantage by customers) should be the source of confidence. Selling is a persuasive art that should be used to motivate the customer logically and emotionally to buy something with which he or she will ultimately be delighted. The customer's ultimate satisfaction is the definitive goal, and unrealistic expectations for a product should neither be created nor allowed to persist, *even if they are generated by the customer*. It requires real strength to caution a potential customer that he or she are setting higher expectations than the product can realistically meet.

Communications Skills

Professional salespeople exhibit effective communications skills. They are proficient in understanding what customers say and the feelings that surround their statements and in energetically and creatively explaining points in terms that customers can understand. They will often defer to the customer and use his or her term for a feature rather than try to educate the customer in the vendor company's terminology and vocabulary. The objective is to increase the customer's comfort with the product, not intimidate or impress the customer with one's own elevated IQ. For this reason, colorful and expressive analogies producing word pictures create comfortable understanding for the customer. It takes energy to communicate effectively and creatively and to simplify a complex concept so that the customer feels comfortable and confident with a product. Salespersons over time develop colorful speech and gestures under the unrelenting pressure to communicate more effectively. They know that "complex is easy" but "simple is an art" – and simple is what sells.

Taste and Judgment

Professional salespeople understand that appearance, including dress, hair style, and posture, all communicate. The objective is not to prove the rampant individuality of the salesperson but to make the customer comfortable that the salesperson is an individual from whom dependable and honorable behavior can be expected. Professional salespeople would much rather prove their individuality with an outstanding paycheck and satisfied customers than with a ring through their nose. The two can be mutually exclusive. An attitude of *deference* sums it up – that is, being willing to submerge one's personal ego in order to offer maximum service to the customer. The object is to help the customer achieve an effective answer and an improved level of happiness by using the product, not for the salesperson to make a personal social statement. Indeed, producing and delivering excellence in product quality that delights customers may in the final analysis be the most appropriate and enduring of all social statements.

The best professional salespeople listen to understand, not just to get the facts but also to gauge the impact of feeling that a deficiency or problem under discussion is causing the customer. This is objective, nonjudgmental listening. This is listening with empathy – genuine concern. Clear communications – listening with interest and concern, sincere personal interest, useful advice, and supportive gestures – all result in a generally likable sales personality. In selling, each individual's unique sales personality is a most valuable asset. It should be constantly improving and expanding toward a more complete credibility as a counselor.

Professional salespeople must be able to engage a range of customers at a peer level. Therefore, the flexibility to fit into a variety of sales situations is important. A highly respected business executive once remarked, "The two things business people should seek in their associates are *taste* and *judgment* – everything else can be bought by the yard." Engagement and partnership at a peer level with executives means taste and judgment are required of salespeople. These are appropriate at all levels of selling.

In summary, commitment perfects individual sales techniques that may be selected from the numerous approaches outlined in texts dealing with such methods. The personality will fit the technique to form a unique sales style for each individual. Most salespeople are open to and enjoy constructive criticism. Professional salespeople know that improved personal characteristics mean improved sales. "A smile and a shoeshine" are still appropriate; they're just not to be relied upon as the essence of selling.

The Customer's Advocate

A company's sales group should be a valuable conduit by which the company comes to understand empathetically the mind of its customers. In designing and manufacturing products that will appeal to customers, this guidance can be crucial. No other approach can so completely confirm the subjective components of customer attitudes. This is because the professional salespeople are artisans in human thought. They may appear to differ amongst themselves, but understanding what customers perceive as value is common to all who are effective. They must have product features and company support that can be presented as maximum value to customers. Their persuasive force is bounded by the realities actually provided by the product. At heart, they are customer advocates attempting to discover and present the product at maximum value in the customer's terms.

Quality Era managers must refine their customer information mechanism by facilitating better internal communications with sales groups. Modifications indicated from information gathered from salespeople may not prove difficult, yet the resulting improvement in customer product acceptance can be substantial. There are mechanisms at work in the marketplace that the sales group can help to interpret. Regardless of company strategy, the sales group can inject sometimes surprising doses of customer-based reality. Today, they often feel excluded. Sales organizations must be included in the gathering and interpretation of customer information for the Quality Era company. They can also introduce customers to design and development groups. Introducing direct customer observations into the product design and development phase can generate enormous benefits. Not doing it can have disastrous results.

The story is told of a company that set out to create a masterpiece of canine nutrition. After the marketing department surveyed the market, the research and development team again verified the requirement and the opportunity. The development group called in the finest specialists in nutrition, aroma, texture, labeling, advertising, and manufacturing. All bases appeared covered, and the fantastic new product was announced to the sales force. With an extravagant sales rally, experts from each of the contributing headquarters came on stage and provided product facts and figures until no more about the product could be told. Thus inspired, the salespeople were sent out to the field to sell the product. Sales results were dismal!

The company president called a second sales meeting. Again, he paraded in the experts, who gave even more facts and figures, and emphasized the fact that this session was to ensure that the sales group got the message – this time, for sure. At the conclusion of the session, the president, clearly in no mood to tolerate negatives, asked the sales audience, several hundred strong, "Is there reason now why you cannot sell this product?" One hand slowly went up from the back row. "And why have you determined that you cannot sell this product?" the president thundered. "Sir," came the reply, "Dogs won't eat the dog food."

Early in a product's development, companies must involve the sales force (the people in contact with the customers) and the customers as well or they proceed at their own peril in the competitive world of quality. The real obstacles to true success in many instances can be erased by simple measures. They are best dealt with in planning phase and not after the cement has been poured. They cannot be dealt with at all if they are not understood by management. Customers cannot be forced to buy anything by a vendor's pure marketing logic. They will do what they want to do.

Summary

Selling has been and will continue to be a challenging profession. It is one that tends to attract individuals who can and must act on their own initiative and who possibly, more than those in most professions, make use of their own personality and communications capabilities.

Most salespeople are quite moral and wish to enjoy the earned esteem of their customers and their company, but selling has historically carried with it a somewhat tarnished image. In reality, selling and the free-market system in which it thrives are responsible for the enormous variety of products that currently benefit mankind.

Professional selling in the Quality Era is demanding consultant-level capabilities and the flexibility and creativity to deal with a variety of situations with competence and credibility. To a degree, salespeople probably work less for their company than for their customers but they must be fair to both. The Quality Era sales group must be capable of creatively structuring the partnership linkages that will become increasingly common between vendors and customers. They must be capable of seeing the larger problems of customers in order to develop and present the more comprehensive product solutions required by the modern era.

Notes

1. It's worth recalling here two of Deming's 14 points – #9, break down barriers and encourage teamwork and #11b, eliminate management by objective – that were discussed in chapter 1.
2. As Deming noted, the objective of business is to delight the customer.

CHAPTER 5

THE BUYING DECISION

Selling in the Quality Era will require a more thorough form of product and company revelation than was required in the past. Up until now, it was the product that was being sold. Quality Era selling is relationship selling – concept selling combined with product selling. The *buying decision* is a comprehensive selling process designed to produce a more thoroughly sold customer, a customer who buys the product concept first and the specific product second, a customer who knows why he or she is buying the product and why he or she will buy from the same vendor in the future. It is a Quality Era selling structure to which continuous quality improvement principles can be applied. The buying decision focuses on empathetic selling; understanding that the decision to buy takes place in the mind of the customer.

The buying decision structure can also serve business management in planning facets of product design and support that will make a product and its company inherently more salable. Businesses must design and build products that can delight the customer, but that kind of satisfaction will not be enjoyed unless the product finds ready acceptance in the market. By reviewing a company's products in regard to the points of the buying decision, guidance can be provided for enhancing the product and for ensuring the ultimate in customer enjoyment.

People actually love to buy! This fact should give continuing confidence to a vendor company and its salespeople. A walk through a mall at Christmas will reveal droves of people actively shopping. They may not appreciate some of the hassle, but they are stimulated by the products and the variety of choices. Buying and shopping are ways of seeking answers to perceived needs. When people are aware of a need and determine that a product represents an answer to that need, they go into acquisition mode and exhibit buying behavior. When they scan the displayed items in the hope of fulfilling needs of which they haven't even been aware, they are in a "just-looking" mode. Shopping can also simply be a search for the most favorable terms of purchase for a specific item.

While people love to shop and to buy, they dislike being "sold" in the sense of having a product pushed upon them, of making a decision they may later regret. One outstanding characteristic of Quality Era selling is that the salesperson will be committed to assisting customers in avoiding postsale disillusionment. Quality Era selling must result in customers who feel that they were not "sold." Such customers will relate that after a brief and helpful discussion with the salesperson, *they* decided to buy. A customer who feels that the decision to buy was all his or her own doing is a supreme mark of a professional sale.

The Quality Era professional salesperson must be aware that people actually enjoy buying and that there is a specific process that can allow them to reach a buying decision comfortably. Whether customers reach this decision on their own or as the result of a personalized sales presentation, they still decide to buy via the same process.

A Natural Decision Process

When an apple is ripe, it falls easily from the tree. When the ingredients of a buying decision are brought together in the mind of the customer, a sale is the natural consequence. An effective salesperson can hasten this process by supplying ingredients at an intensified rate instead of waiting for nature to take its course. The high-pressure, conquest, or encounter-oriented selling techniques of the past were ethically questionable – because they were attempts to shortchange nature and pick the apple too early, before all the proper ingredients were present. Sales that are made without all the proper elements have negative consequences: They don't stick!

Quality Era selling has a three fold objective in the creation of buying decisions: (1) Customers obtain solutions to their needs, gaining lasting satisfaction from the product purchased; (2) This secures a lasting relationship between the customer and the salesperson's company; (3) These customers tell other potential customers of their satisfaction with the company and its product.[1]

The decision to buy results from a specific group of elements coming into clear focus in the mind of the customer. The Quality Era salesperson will organize a discussion that brings these elements or building blocks into position. The decision to buy can thus be considered as an action resulting from a completed mental construction. This is not some form of automated, never-fail selling, because it may be found that for a particular customer the construction cannot be properly made for a particular product. However, if the construction can be made, the customer can be expected to buy.

Let's take a brief look at the elements of a buying decision and then review them in more detail. The fundamental elements of the buying decision are *need,* followed closely by *desire.* A need must be recognized and confirmed by both the salesperson and the customer. Quality Era salespeople never sell to a nonexistent need. Once the need is established, desire can be created and/or intensified. Desire takes the form of a decision by the customer to take action, to obtain the item, or to listen with increased, genuine interest as the sales discussion proceeds.

Once need and desire are established, the salesperson must help the prospect to see that buying the product is a sound, rational decision. This third element is called *justification;* it often involves financial considerations. Its object is to give the customer a reasonable cause to buy once all the implications of the decision have been considered.

Education is the fourth element. The salesperson must help the customer develop a conceptual understanding of how the component parts and design qualities of the product contribute to its overall function and beneficial performance.

Finally, *implementation* must be discussed; this means ensuring that the customer can visualize how the product or service can be installed or implemented with a minimum amount of disruption. (A part of any real cure is the requirement that it not kill the patient.)

When each of these components is in place, the customer

will make a decision to buy. But the mortar that holds the salesperson's construction together is *credibility* (see Figure 5.1). Credibility ensures that as each element or block is laid in place, the image of the salesperson and the company as honest, understanding, and knowledgeable will increase. At all points, the salesperson must be able to honestly and accurately substantiate his or her claims for the product. There must be no overstatement of results or product capability. A slip in honesty or integrity during the construction can cost the sale and the loss of a future relationship. Honest mistakes can be made; they can be corrected and forgiven. It is the perception of actual dishonesty that is fatal.

Quality Era professional salesmanship makes use of a variety of "tools" in the construction of buying decisions. The proper sales technique or tool is selected to add or firm up blocks as the sales effort progresses. For example, education (the requirement to conceptually understand the working of a product and its component features) can be clarified through a product demonstration. The response of a fire alarm to smoke or the ability of a fire extinguisher to quickly eliminate a blaze can visibly clarify their concept and function. Credibility is also enhanced as the product's capabilities are confirmed through demonstration. Having outlined the components of the buying decision, a closer look at each of the component elements is in order.

Need

Psychologists have called humans "need-driven animals." Studies of human behavior suggest that we are preoccupied with satisfying our perceived needs. Buying behavior is certainly such an attempt.

But what are "needs"? Many attempts have been made to define the term, most of which have concluded that needs are deficiencies, gaps, a lack of something judged or felt to be essential. When a person perceives that some essential emotional or tangible aspect of his or her life is not at a satisfactory level, a gap exists – a discrepancy. There is a distance between where the person *is* in regard to that aspect and where he or she *would like to be*. The size of the gap represents the magnitude

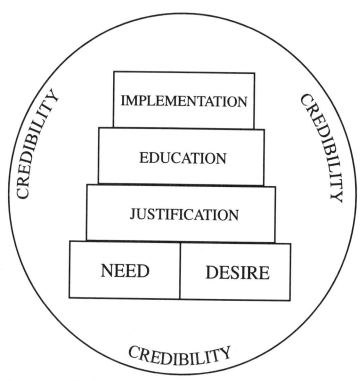

Figure 5.1. The buying decision is a construction of essential elements bound together by the mortar of credibility, which, when put together properly, produces a proper Quality Era sale.

of the need. Human behavior, including buying behavior, can often be predicted if the customer's greatest needs are understood. At any moment, an individual's actions are probably oriented toward reducing the magnitude of his or her greatest perceived need.

The following are examples of some areas in which basic needs exist:

Emotional	*Physical*
Love	Food
Security	Clothing

Self-respect	Shelter
Power	Safety
Self-expression	Self-preservation
Pleasure	Avoidance of pain

Notice that each of these areas allows for the possibility of two aspects of need. The first need is to gain more (i.e., establish a better state) and the second is to avoid losing what is presently held (i.e., create a worse situation). In terms of our need fulfillment, we tend to behave so as to hold on to the degree of need satisfaction we have achieved while attempting to gain more in areas where we perceive a deficiency. Such deficiencies are always present, for, as Adam Smith observed, man is the dissatisfied animal.[2]

An unfulfilled need manifests itself in terms of emotional tension – a form of internal emotional pressure. The human mind surveys the present situation and seeks to determine what factors are causing these tensions. Once a cause is identified, the mind moves to develop a plan satisfying the need – that is, reducing the gap – or reducing that need to a level where the tension is more acceptable. Since human behavior is based on reducing many needs, only those of a certain magnitude result in action. *A need perceived as mild is not a motivator.* It will not produce action or overt buying behavior.

The form of behavior of most interest to professional salespeople is buying behavior, the acquisition of an item or service that a customer perceives will satisfy or diminish a need. Thus the decision to buy must ultimately be the customer's own, clear plan. The professional salesperson helps the customer develop the plan. Empathy allows salespeople to put themselves in the rational and emotional place of the customer to formulate appropriate solutions to that customer's needs. Salespeople who lack such empathy are in essence blind to development of appropriate customer solutions. Just as movie actors place themselves in the role of a scripted character, salespeople must place themselves in the role of the customer.

The desire to satisfy one need can cause tension in another area. For example, acquiring a new dress can be perceived by a buyer as satisfying a need for positive self-image or acceptance, but it can reduce satisfaction in the area of her need for financial security, which is presently being satisfied by a healthy bank account. The mind seeks to determine a behavior pattern over the whole of the individual's needs spectrum that will result in a net plus result. That is, more tension must be reduced in buying the dress than is going to be produced reducing the bank balance. With an impinging multiplicity of needs, it is easy to see that the mind stays continually busy making these evaluations and in reconciling needs with opportunity.

In searching for answers to needs, the mind uses a particular process – *visualization*. The human mind uses visualization both to determine sources of tension and also in formulating its plans to eliminate them. As we mentally picture our situation, tensions rise and fall within us. When we imagine the future or recall situations from our past, we find that our *emotions* color the picture.

For example, when we remember an embarrassing incident, we feel a twinge of emotion along with a mental picture as we recall the event. If we think about the possibility that in tomorrow's conference we may be required to stand up and give a brief summary about ourselves, that picture will also be accompanied by another emotion (possibly mild apprehension). Since we want to avoid tension in our lives, we may try to limit the possibility of having to perform an activity mentally perceived as leading to increased anxiety. Through visualization we can formulate behavioral plans that allow us to avoid or minimize the troubling situation and the resulting tension. Likewise, we can imagine a great number of situations we could be involved in that would reduce tension and lead to pleasure.

This same principle holds true when we consider buying and owning an item. Whether or not this mental picture is emotionally pleasing to us determines our level of interest and our motivation to acquire it. Thus, we derive a pivotal rule of buying behavior: *People buy according to the feelings that result from visualizing themselves using or possessing the product.* To the degree that the emotions produced by these visualizations are increasingly pleasurable and effectively seem to satisfy great needs, the will to obtain or reject the object will be intensified. Thus, "the regulation of the purse is, in its essence, regulation of the imagination and the heart." (Ruskin, *Unto This Last*, 176)

What we have just discussed relates to the first element of the buying decision – need – in the following manner: The mind constantly considers many alternative causes of the tensions it is experiencing. It is seeking to define the sources of its tension in order to develop a plan to reduce it. It is at this point that the salesperson can be of assistance.

The salesperson seeking to find a buyer for a product must seek those persons who have real needs that can be met by the product. It's an old and rather bad joke that a really good salesperson "could sell refrigerators to Eskimos." A Quality Era salesperson would do a more accurate job of identifying prospects who truly needed the product. As Deming stated, the objective is to create customer delight. Disillusionment is produced when we are persuaded to buy something for which we later realize we had no need.

The professional salesperson will be seen by the customer at the beginning of a sales discussion as assisting in identifying areas of need with which the customer agrees. The salesperson will also demonstrate that he or she understands the need – the problem as the customer *sees* it and *feels* it. This is a most powerful vantage point, for the unempathetic cannot establish this level of caring identity with a customer.

A professional salesperson will not attempt to create need where none exists. This is not solving a problem; it is creating one. Quality Era salesmanship will instead often help to uncover legitimate needs that were not apparent to the customer. Problems often appear to us as *symptoms* rather than as clear-cut problems. Just as a physician sometimes shows us that seemingly unrelated symptoms are caused by a single, underlying malady, so professional salespersons seek to understand the real needs producing the symptoms outlined by their customers.

In determining need through discussion a general picture of *conceptual solution* should begin to emerge. Discussion of the conceptual solution and its required characterictics is a much lower threat approach than going immediately to a *specific* product solution. The need therefore requires a certain conceptual answer, and once the customer agrees in concept the specific product can be presented as the answer to conceptual requirements for a solution.

If no realistic need for an available product can be uncovered for the customer, the salesperson should not continue with the sales construction. He or she should, if possible, recommend another product or approach that might solve the customer's problem. Professional salespeople do not attempt to hammer square pegs into round holes. As John Ruskin reminded us, "Honesty in business may be in itself a sufficiently worthy objective." (*Unto This Last*, 110) The Quality Era demands that credibility never be sacrificed just to make a sale.

Desire

People do not always buy what they rationally need; they buy what they want! When needs become so intense and immediate as to demand a solution, they have become wants. An emotional want of an intensity sufficient to cause a prospect to take action to acquire the product is called desire.

In selling, desire is created most effectively by enabling the prospect to clearly visualize possession and use of the product. In the imagined situation, he or she is experiencing a feeling of intensified satisfaction in the need areas, which are producing high tension under their present unsatisfied condition.

Here is an example. As John Clark drove his 1988 Chevrolet down Main Street last night, he stopped at the red light at 4th and Main.

"If this car makes it for one more month, I'll be lucky," he thought to himself. "It really is reaching the limits – using too much oil, transmission slipping; I really doubt whether it's completely safe." Just at that instant, John happened to glance out his right window, and his eye caught the shiny, new BMW convertible sitting in the showroom on the corner.

"Boy, what a car," he thought. "If I had that, what a time I'd have. Saturdays I'd get up at 7:30, and Cindy and I could get out of town before the traffic gets heavy. It would be super driving out toward the mountains in that cool morning air with the top down, the cool wind in my face, that engine purring along. What control. The steering is outstanding. Leather seats, too. This is one fine car. Picnic by the stream, water on the rocks, total relaxation, back in the car – that transmission is as smooth as silk. Time to get back – sunset – beautiful orange on those clouds – gorgeous as it shines down across the hood and sort of sparkles off the front."

Cindy pats the top of the dash: "John, it's just wonderful." (Pop!) I'm going to stop in tomorrow and talk to those folks, he resolved.

Professional salespeople realize that dreams are more powerful than reality, for perfection can exist in dreams. It is rare in reality. Salespeople often must help their prospects to "see" (i.e., visualize and understand) the actual problems of their present circumstance. They must use this visualization to contrast these circumstances with the improved situation that could exist if the customer obtained the salesperson's product.

As we all know, dreams can be shattered by reality. The salesperson must not overdramatize the problems with the customer's present reality nor make the promise of the new situation unrealistic. But the salesperson should, as powerfully and effectively as possible, draw an accurate contrast between these two sets of circumstances for the customer. When creating these visualizations, the salesperson should be sensitive to the customer's needs and attitudes rather than focused on personal ones. What may be pleasing for the salesperson may not be appealing to the customer. For example, a youthful salesperson's emphasis on the outstanding heavy bass response of a stereophonic sound system might be inappropriate for an elderly customer with a preference for classical music and a decline in high tone hearing capacity.

Desire is created by offering the customer two contrasting visualizations – the old way (fraught with problems and frustrations that lead to increased tension) and the new way (filled with advantages and benefits that will relieve tension). The buyer will seek to get from the old over to the new; the product is the "bridge." Desire makes the buyer want to cross over; just as weather patterns move from high pressure to low, people buy to move to a better state with lessened tension. Adam Smith's desire for betterment is at work today as always. See Figure 5.2.

Justification

The professional salesperson will now help the prospect to make the trip across that bridge. We all see things that we want, but we often hesitate because we are mature, *rational* adults. We know that dreams are powerful and elicit forceful "wants," but we must be "practical." John may be intense in his desire for the BMW right now, but in the morning, when he sees the price and thinks of the impact on his savings, he may not decide to buy. The salesperson for the auto agency, however, may be able to show John from another perspective that when he buys the car he is really making an investment that, when costs over the life of the car and high trade-in value are considered, is actually not as costly as he may have thought. When the monthly cost of maintaining his old car is taken into consideration along with its lack of safety, the purchase price may not seem so threatening. And when the financing plan over four years is tailored to John's income, there may be a way that he can affordably get what he wants.

The salesperson should present all the reasons why the decision is positive and why John can possibly afford to buy. The salesperson should be truly objective because, if results are not as presented, John will be disillusioned (unmet expectations) later. After all the evidence for what John wants to do represents a sound decision has been thoroughly presented, John must make up his own mind. The salesperson's role is to assist John in comprehensively recognizing and analyzing all aspects of justification.

Education

Educating the customer to help him or her appreciate the value that differentiates a product from its competition is a most important Quality Era concept. Value is based on the worth (i.e., the personal usefulness) of a product as perceived by the customer. Value is also the relationship between the benefits cus-

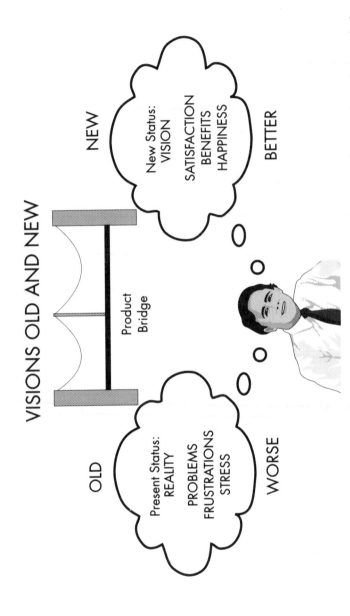

Figure 5.2. The visualization of an improved status through possession of the product produces buying behavior.

tomers "see" themselves obtaining and what must be given up to obtain them. When an item is perceived to offer more benefit to a customer than must be given up to acquire it, then the item is perceived to have a net positive value.

In the buying decision, education serves two distinct purposes: it gives the prospect a conceptual understanding of the product's workings and the quality of its design. Prospects can then visualize how the claims made for the product can actually be realized, which heightens their appreciation of the product's quality (its positive value) *and* removes the fear of buying something unknown by reassuring them that they can manage, control, or effectively use it.

The ability of a salesperson to explain the design characteristics and thoughtful craftsmanship that went into the product reflects on his or her professionalism and that of the company. Thorough product design knowledge is always an attribute of a professional salesperson. With each sale, he or she imparts to the customer sufficient understanding of the design and functioning of the product to allow him or her to fully appreciate the product and to allay any fears they might have about it. A concern for customers shown through a product's quality communicates the integrity of its maker. This wins the respect of the customer for the manufacturer or vendor beyond the product level. It builds toward trust and partnership.

Creativity in explaining a product can comfort a prospect greatly. Often *analogous* explanations (using an item or process with which the prospect is already comfortable) are the best way to explain a concept. As an example, a new computer customer might ask, "How does a program work?" You could say, "A computer program is a set of software instructions or steps which the computer executes in processing information. The user puts information (data) into the computer (input); the computer processes it according to the steps in the program, and the result is output to printer, CRT, or other output device."

Or, you might say, "Do you have a washing machine? Does it have several cycles for washing different loads of clothes? Each of the cycles is a program containing a set of instructions, such as fill, wash, rinse, spin. At the end dirty clothes are clean

– right? The computer program is similar to the washing machine, except that information is put in – or processed – according to the specific steps prescribed by the program and then comes out in another arrangement as a result of the process."

The salesperson who discussed computer programming in terms of the washing machine might sell more computers to apprehensive customers. The objective is not to impress the customer with how complex the product is, but to reduce it to an understandable and therefore manageable concept. As one old sales manager once said of jargon and verbal overkill, "Samson slew a thousand Philistines with the jawbone of an ass[3] – and thousands of sales are killed every day with the same instrument." Salespeople need to remember to clarify, not obfuscate.

The salesperson's analogies need not be precisely accurate, but it should be sufficiently appropriate so that the customer will not be misled in understanding and using the product. Selling a product is really an educational challenge. The prospect needs to understand the product's features and benefits as the salesperson sees them. Getting another individual to perceive what we perceive is essentially educating them about our point of view.

Let's return to our example of John and his BMW. John has just reviewed the payment schedule with an air of finality saying,

"I just may be able to do it. This payment plan fits my budget."

"Shall I write up the contracts, then?" asks the salesman.

"Well, it's still a big decision. I've never owned a foreign car before." The salesman senses John's concern.

"Many people have an initial apprehension about owning a foreign automobile. For a realistic look at the situation, let's go back to our service department," the salesman says. John walks out on the service floor with the salesman and is introduced to the service manager, Bob Sutton.

"Bob, John is considering the new convertible in the showroom and has some concern about the car's being foreign – repairs, service, and the like."

Bob smiles. "A very good point," he says. "Serviceability is essential with anything mechanical. Let me show you why you have nothing to worry about from that aspect. Let's start over here – this is a 1983 model. Look at the odometer mileage."

John looks in the window – 231,000! "Is that correct?"

"You bet," says Bob. "These cars are built to last. Let me show you something else." He takes the service log from the windshield and opens it.

"That's why," he says. Outlined in the log is a check mark by each of the service intervals, going all the way back to the 1983 purchase date. "Get yours serviced as we prescribe, and you can expect the same. Look over here. This one is attached to our computer diagnostic center." John is impressed by the wires leading out of the car's engine compartment and over to the panel covered with a complicated array of dials and displays.

"You are looking at the most sophisticated diagnostic technique available," says Bob. "We check the car out every time you come in for service. The intent is to detect problems before they start. We feel that this is not a foreign car, but rather a quality car. Only the added degree of attention to detail, craftsmanship in construction, engineering, and service is foreign. We keep a complete stock of parts here. Should we happen to be out of an item, we receive three air shipments each week from our distribution center, and even next-morning delivery is available in an emergency."

John says, "I feel better about service."

"Let's look through this booklet of illustrations showing the design features and engineering innovations incorporated in a BMW," suggests the salesman. "It does a very good job of explaining the car and its manufacture. It will help show you exactly what you are getting for your money and why a BMW performs and lasts so well."

Implementation

Implementation involves developing and presenting an acceptable plan of putting the product into use. When this point in the buying decision is reached, professional salespeople will creatively assist the customer in visualizing how the product can be put to use quickly and with minimal effort. Let's return to John's story to see how this can be done.

"I like the car," says John.

"I know you do," replies the salesman. "Would you like to pick it up this afternoon?"

"Can you get it ready that fast?"

The salesman says he can. "It will require my 'walking it through,' but I'll do that for you. Just come back at 4:00 and I'll have everything ready. Be sure to get everything out of the old car so you can leave it with us." (A complete rejection of the "old" – the beginning of a new life.)

"There is one more problem," says John.

"What's that?"

"Where will I keep it?" asks John.

"Don't you have a garage?"

"Yes, but I have a small workbench that takes up part of the garage space."

"Are you going to let a small workbench stand in the way of *years* of driving pleasure?" asks the salesman. (There are some problems dealing with implementation that customers often will just have to solve for themselves.)

"I guess not," John replies.

"Let's sign the agreements," said the salesman.

So John buys the car. He has completed the buying decision with the salesman's help and, because his expectations have been kept at a reasonable level by the salesman, he will enjoy the car and be glad that he bought it.

A salesperson quite often has to begin by uncovering and confirming a need and creating desire. After that, he or she can proceed on through the whole cycle. In this case, need and desire were already present and the salesman's job was simplified. He constructed the justification, education, and implementation aspects of the buying decision.

A key point to remember is that a salesperson must understand where a customer is in the construction of the buying decision and then assist him or her in putting the missing blocks in place. John has made a buying decision. He was assisted in its construction by a professional, caring, and empathetic salesperson and the BMW agency has a new and loyal customer.

Quality Era buying decisions should be constructed by following this plan. The visions held out by professional salespeople lead the public forward to a better life in the free-enterprise system. Buying and selling conducted honestly are enjoyable social interchanges that add spice to life.

Proposals and Closing

Even though a sales discussion is proceeding with ease and speed – the customer has agreed that there is a specific need, expressed a willingness to make a change, confirmed that the product's value to him exceeds its price, come to an understanding of the concepts of product function, and agreed to a practical plan to implement the product – someone must state the obvious: "It's time to buy!" The individual who most often recognizes when this point has been reached is the salesperson. It is time to close the sale.

When the buying decision has been completely developed, the close will be a natural and logical consequence – almost the answer to the question, "What comes next?"

The salesperson may feel that the job is complete, having gained affirmative responses to all components of the buying decision. If the customer agrees to all the parts, then they must agree to the whole construction, right? Wrong! Customers always have the right to change their mind and must be given the opportunity to voice an objection to any point at any time. Remember that a sales discussion may have spanned some time – even multiple visits. Points that were clear some time ago may be less clear now. There needs to be a concise summation of points agreed to on each component of the buying decision and then a logical request for the order. The purpose of this summary is to answer any remaining questions and to bring into clear focus all of the elements of the buying decision. With each element in clear focus, a decision can be made to buy.

Depending on the type of product and the sales situation, this summary can take several forms. It can be verbal, with the salesperson restating the important issues discussed within each element of the buying decision and the conclusion reached and agreed to by the prospect at each point. Restating and seeking agreement builds confidence in the customer that the problem and its solution are understood and perceived correctly by the salesperson.

Objections

Customers will voice occasional doubts or concerns during sales discussions that were not anticipated and addressed by the salesperson. These are traditionally called *objections*, but they are simply concerns voiced as questions. They should always be seen as questions by the salesperson. For instance, a comment like, "The whizbang you're selling costs too much!" should be heard by the salesperson as, "Why again is this whizbang going to produce benefits to me that exceed the price you are asking?" The salesperson needs to revisit the need and justification areas of the buying decision. Objections should be expected and answered; they are a positive sign that the customer is mentally reviewing the buying decision for incomplete or hazy elements. If these can be clarified, there is a potential sale. The salesperson should touch on each element and ask if the recommended product fits this particular customer in terms of need, desire, justification, education, and implementation. Credibility is built based on how honestly and thoroughly the salesperson has discussed the other elements.

Customer objections should be noted as the discussion moves through the buying decision and answered satisfactorily when each buying decision element is touched upon. There should be a restatement of objections in a concluding statement that succinctly states the customer's position – that is, "As I understand your concerns, Mr. Adams, you are concerned that the whizbang may possibly be too large for your closet and that it possibly costs too much."

Get agreement. Limit the objections by confirming that these two concerns are *all* that really keeps Mr. Adams from buying the whizbang. If this is true, then the salesperson has only *two* questions to resolve to get the order. An open discussion of the issues is the only route to a solid sale and future trust. The product must ultimately be found to exceed customer expectations if it is to create delight. Forcing a fit to get an order is not appropriate. Creativity and an innovative approach are appropriate in resolving objections, but the product will be evaluated in actual use, and that is where delight will be measured. Following the format of the buying decision is as appropriate for retail sales as for the largest real estate deal, though in the retail situation the elements will be moved through very quickly. The format is applicable to any sales situation, although the energy and detail applied must be appropriate to the situation.

Written Proposals

The professional sales close can be summarized in a written proposal. Written proposals have been downplayed in recent years in many professional personal selling organizations – in many cases, this has been due to the absurd nature of the proposals being generated. Many were too wordy, with excessive jargon. As one salesperson commented some years back, "You would think that business decisions were being made based on the physical weight of the proposals rather than on the logic of the business case being put forward."

The concept that very few top decision makers will take time to read dozens of pages of detail in making a product decision is essentially correct. But we are not talking about that type of proposal here; we are talking about a different concept in proposal development that can assist Quality Era businesses in selling more and in developing the talents of their sales personnel – proposals that clarify the elements of the buying decision and lead to solid expectations that will be met and exceeded by the product. Created and presented properly, these instruments confirm the professionalism of the salesperson and the company.

Quality Era Proposals

In personal professional selling situations, where appropriate, a brief written proposal should be delivered *and reviewed with prospects* as a closing technique. The proposal should be brief, direct, and structured to follow the buying decision. It should use the prospect's own vocabulary and numerical data.

Such proposals do several things, all of which are powerful. They clarify the buying decision elements so that a decision to buy can be made. They set criteria for the expected performance of the product as a solution implemented. They can be referenced to check actual results as compared to expectations. They serve as a guide for the actual development of a sales approach by ensuring that sales personnel design complete sales arguments in line with the buying decision. They provide sales and other management with a concise view of the sales arguments that are being presented by sales for the products being sold, and also outline customer problems as perceived by customers. All of these are highly useful and of significance in Quality Era selling. Let's consider an example of what a Quality Era proposal might look like:

Mr. John B. Wilkerson
President
Ace Widget Company
2700 Industrial Drive
Anytown, USA 242424

Dear Mr. Wilkerson:

Thank you for the cordial welcome you afforded me last Wednesday and for the enlightening and candid discussion in which we engaged. I believe that as a result of that visit we have a comprehensive understanding of the challenges that you face in manufacturing widgets and, in particular, feel that we can recommend a complete answer to the widget manufacturing problems that plague your present approach.

You indicated that the most important shortfall of the present widget-making machine is its lack of production volume and, as you indicated after a review of throughput by your production supervisor, that the equipment, though old, is still producing widgets at close to capacity. Tolerances have slipped irreparably since the machine was originally purchased in 1982.

The present machine has served you well but now produces insufficient quantity and inferior-quality widgets. You are missing orders and generating customer complaints of inconsistent quality and failure to meet your published delivery schedules. You need to make a change; your present equipment will not meet your stated objectives of quality and volume. Based on your figures, we determined that the loss of revenue in February was $10,000; with your standard widget margin of 40 percent, this equates to a loss of $4,000 profit in that month alone.

You indicated that customer complaints regarding care quality have had an impact, possibly as great as those due to lost revenue. Mr. Smith, your customer relations supervisor, commented that he receives at least two customer calls per week regarding poor quality. Customers are being affected, your business image is being tarnished, and productive work time is being lost as your employees address quality complaint issues. You feel that it is time to change, and we agree.

If only the factor of lost gross profit is used at the figure of $4,000 per month, an annual payment stream of $48,000 could be applied to obtain a satisfactory solution. This figure includes no monies lost in customer goodwill due to quality and order slippage and none also for time and attitude impact on your employees answering quality and delivery problems for customers.

As we discussed, there are several methods of answering your need. You indicated that you desire an output volume from any new widget machine of at least 50 percent above that of the old machine. Reviews of several approaches, including obtaining a second older machine, were considered, but personnel expense and the quality improvement issues make this unacceptable. After a thorough discussion of all surrounding issues, we arrived at the conclusion that our new "Widget Maker Deluxe" is clearly the best solution. It offers flexible, widget-bending capability based on the new hydraulic unit, which can be reset continuously throughout the life of the equipment to bring dimensions back on target in regard to quality. This fine new machine seems expensive at first, but when viewed with a 10-year life cycle cost analysis and its flexibility to meet your changing requirements, it offers a most cost-effective solution.

Its $100,000 cost can be defrayed over five years at your

current bank rate of 7 percent. You and your accountant will easily see that when depreciation and our offer of $15,000 for your old equipment is considered, financially the decision is a sound one, considering that meeting this obligation can easily be covered using the $4,000 monthly net profit realized from increased production. This does not include improvement in customer service, the perceived quality improvement evident to your customers, and the attitudinal improvement on the part of your workers, who will be proud of the new widgets and their ability to deliver them.

We have visited with our engineers concerning installation of your new equipment and find that the time frame you mentioned as desirable (June 7–9) can be reserved for you. If your people will make the old machine available beginning at 7:00 a.m. on June 7, our engineers will remove the old machine and replace it with the new one by 7:30 p.m. June 8. In the meantime, we have arranged for Mr. Phil Donovan, your machine operator, to receive on-site training in the use of the new equipment at Ajax Industries here in town. Thus, the new machine will be in place and in production after only two days of down time on your part, and thereafter you can move on to other issues because you will have answered the widget issue that is causing you such concern at present.

We look forward to working with you to realize your fullest expectations regarding both installation and performance of our equipment. We count it a privilege to be able to serve you, to work with you and your company, and to be a part of your future success. We have carefully reviewed our capabilities and those of our equipment in regard to meeting all the needs you have listed. We welcome the opportunity to serve you in this matter. Your signature on the enclosed Equipment Purchase Agreement will allow us to begin working on your June 7 installation.

Sincerely,

Joseph A. Smith
Sales Representative

Arthur Coleman
President
ABC Machine Tool Company

The example, you will notice, follows the buying decision construction format. Generating a written proposal prompts the salesperson to consider the logical impact of the total sales argument. If the salesperson cannot form and present clear and organized reasons why a customer should buy, then those reasons may certainly remain unclear to the customer. Clarify and state the obvious facts: If the customer has assisted in the construction of the buying decision, he or she will recognize the validity of the proposal, which is a written summarization of their own situation and opinions. It is the customer who has the need; the salesperson helps organize the issues so that both the problem and its implications – and the solution and its advantages – are clearly presented and perceived. The requirement to present a brief but clearly organized proposal causes the salesperson to ask the important customer questions and to develop the buying decision properly. The form each point of the proposal takes will vary with situation and salesperson, but the proposal must reconstruct the buying decision elements in a concise and direct manner.

Such a proposal serves to create a benchmark for postsale visits to compare the actual results with those that were anticipated at the time of sale. Salespeople must not be afraid to face the actual results brought about by the products they have recommended. Customers will forgive honest errors and unforeseen difficulties that can affect actual performance if it approximates their expectations. What they will not forgive is dishonesty – credibility lost due to hyperbole of claim and service that does not correspond with what was promised. Retaining a customer depends on meaning what you say and saying what you mean – walking the walk, not just talking the talk. Quality Era selling is commitment to real customer delight, not just the creation of hyped anticipation.

Many personal professional selling situations span more than one sales call or visit. In evaluating the progress in the construction of a buying decision, the following questions might be used to gauge the prospect's status in that process. These points also serve to gauge the level of salesperson and/or customer understanding of each point, which is necessary for a solid buying decision to be constructed. They are questions sales-people should ask themselves or that management can discuss with the salesperson in regard to a particular sales opportunity. In revealing the required depth of understanding of each point of the buying decision, they may also serve to show management as well as the design and production teams the characteristics that must be built into the products.

Summary

The following are the questions that the salesperson should ask him or herself when helping the prospect construct the stages of the buying decision. They encourage a complete empathetic understanding of the customer situation and indicate how clearly the buying decision elements have been established.

Need
What *specific* points of dissatisfaction with the present approach has the prospect voiced or agreed to? What are the *specific* negative consequences that would result if the customer does not change the present approach?

Desire
Why does the sales prospect wish to continue the discussion or evaluation of a new approach? Or, conversely, why doesn't the customer want to continue such a discussion?

Justification
In what specific areas has the customer agreed that money will be saved? (These should be listed or quantified somehow.) What *specific* value has the customer assigned to intangible benefits such as freedom from worry, convenience, safety, and so forth? (Again, these should be quantified.)

Education
Is the sales prospect prepared to explain to a friend or associate how the features of the product will interact to produce benefi-

cial results for him or her? Can the customer explain essentially how the product functions?

Implementation

Is the customer discussing specific names, dates, and schedules in regard to implementation? Does the customer express undue concern in discussing the hassle of implementation?

Credibility

Does the customer seem willing to make time available to visit with the salesperson? Does the customer willingly introduce the salesperson to peers and superiors? Has the customer checked the references or information sources the salesperson has suggested?

The buying decision is a logically structured process by which customers can decide to buy. The decision to buy is made in the mind of the customer. This approach to selling builds salesperson credibility because it anticipates the logical questions that customers will ask when considering a purchase and provides strategy for answering them. This heightens the customer's appreciation of the salesperson's empathy.

The buying decision ensures that sales are based on a thorough understanding of a confirmed need and followed by the development of desire through a review of the benefits of acquiring the product and the possible negative implications of not doing so. Justification helps the customer see the logical support for a decision to buy. Education then explains the product concept to increase appreciation of its quality and confidence in its function and manageability. Anticipating and answering implementation concerns then demonstrate how the vendor will support the customer's ability to put the product in use and realize its benefits. By empathetically and thoroughly uncovering need, the salesperson can differentiate both the product and company from the competition. Customers sold through this methodology are confident they have made the right decision through the help of a truly professional salesperson. As this structure is followed and mixed with the individual talents of salespeople, a continuous process of quality improvement can take place, leading to more success in selling and in delighting customers.

Notes

1. Deming says quality is what keeps customers coming back again and again and again.
2. Abraham Maslow, a noted psychologist, developed a hierarchy of needs going from basic, or physiologic, up to higher level emotional needs, with the highest being self-actualization. His writings on needs can benefit any student of the sales process.
3. Judges 15:15.

CHAPTER 6

THE SALES CONTINUUM

The buying decision should be viewed as the central focus of a process that can be called the *sales continuum*. For too long and in too many businesses, the selling function has been viewed too narrowly, with emphasis given only to a single immediate sale. When seen from a broader perspective, a more complete view of selling as a process takes shape, allowing us to observe an interrelation of stages within the process and to identify specific activities that should take place at each stage. The benefits of this process view also can provide new points of measurement, quality control, and quality improvement.

This perspective of selling as a process includes stages of production. It can and should be equated to a manufacturing process in which the input is raw material and the output is a quality finished product. In the case of the sales continuum, we deal with sales craftsmanship applied to human need and individual personalities to ultimately produce a delighted customer who views the company as the traditional source of product and who sells others on the vendor company and its products.

The sales continuum has two major segments. The first part might be called *engagement*. As shown in Table 6.1, our chart of the sales continuum, this phase spans the area from "Names" to "Buying Decision." In this initial phase, some *names* are selected and moved forward as *suspects*; some suspects are selected and moved forward as *prospects*. Definite process actions are required to move a name forward to receive attention at the next stage. If the in-process item, individual, or account is judged not suitable for the next stage, it is not rejected but simply put on hold under the label of the highest stage it has reached in the process. A visual representation of this process is given in Figure 6.1.

Table 6.1. The selling stages of the sales continuum process

Input	Operation	Output
Names	+ Judgment	= Suspects
Suspects	+ Qualification	= Prospects
Prospects	+ Buying decision/ proposal	= New customer
New customer	+ Support/ Service	= Delighted customer
Delighted customer	+ partnership linkage	= Selling customer

The second phase of the overall process, *retention*, includes the stages from "Buying decision" to "Delighted customer" and utilizes finishing- and polishing-type activities that produce the desired end product: the *delighted and selling customer.*

The sales process we will now outline certainly applies most readily to direct personal selling, but it has applicability to almost all selling situations. All customers must move through it, though the selling of some products warrants less time on each stage.

Let us take a detailed look at each stage of the process in terms of its input, the operations performed, and the end result, or output. Some of the stages of the process may seem obvious and their operation simple. Be assured, however, that a close look at each stage and a thorough understanding of each operation is absolutely key to the achievement of quality in the selling process. Many inefficiencies inherent in present sales approaches result from an improper labeling of individuals within the process. Because individuals are improperly labeled, the operations for which they are scheduled are out of sequence and thus inappropriate, wasting time and efficiency. The key to quality selling is to understand precisely at which stage a client is within the continuum. When this is known, the salesperson will know what operation comes next. It will also be seen that

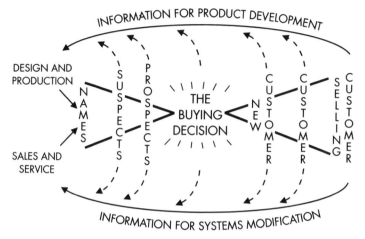

Figure 6.1. The sales continuum. As sales contacts are made from names to "selling customers", information flows back through at all points.

correctly labeled individuals at some stages have much more potential than others at other stages. Sales time and energy can and must be directed toward those situations that offer the greatest potential return in time and energy investment. Proper prioritization of potential sales activity is the key to efficiency and productivity.

Names

Regardless of the product or service sold, literally anyone could be a candidate for a sale. But some are certainly better candidates than others. Why is this? As we contemplate this question, we see that a priority, or hierarchy of probability, begins to emerge. This hierarchy depends on the product and what it offers and on the candidates for a sale and what they need or can find useful. There are vast numbers of candidates out in the world, individuals and businesses who could potentially buy a given product. Reason, or judgment, tells us that not all of them will.

Imagine for a moment a truck salesperson's first day on the job. The sales manager says, "Go out there and sell!" The novice innocently asks him where and to whom. The manager hands over a telephone book and says, "The people who will buy are listed in here." "But," the recruit asks, "which ones are they?" He might reply, "You are the salesperson. That is what I want *you* to find out." The telephone book is several inches thick. No one person could contact everyone listed – at least not fast enough to sell enough trucks to meet his or her quota.

This example illustrates what is meant by the term *names* in the sales continuum process. The telephone book represents a list of names. Names frequently are available to salespersons in the form of lists. The point to be made is that as we look at the entire range of potential buyers for a product, some have characteristics that make them more probable sales candidates than others. We will find that as we understand which individuals in the list of names have business or personal characteristics that we rationally and empathetically deem will make them candidates to need a truck, we will begin to *suspect* a potential need to buy and own a truck (or whatever the product to be sold).

The best candidates to buy a truck from the list of names are, of course, those individuals in need of a truck. Note how creativity, empathy, and judgment spring into action to help sift or filter out those who have probable need from those who probably don't. We learned in our discussion of the buying decision that a satisfied need is not a motivator. We have also noted that people do not simply buy an object – they buy an anticipatory feeling of satisfaction that indicates the product will answer a need or solve a problem. People don't usually buy a truck for its own sake; most buy such a vehicle to haul things. Certain types of objects are best moved around in a truck and, when a truck has been mentally selected from other vehicle types and potential hauling options, the person will be in a buying mode for a truck.

Need, one must remember, cannot be created, although it

can be very creatively uncovered. The essential point of this discussion is that to be most efficient, salespeople must, through judgment and with empathy, prioritize their activity toward those individuals with the highest probability to have a need and thus to buy. These persons have sometimes already come to this realization themselves or are open to be shown that they have a realistic need for the product.

Ethically, it must be emphasized at this point that a salesperson's job is not to sell everyone. The desire to sell everyone, regardless of real need, diverts many salespeople from those who have real product need. Time and talent are the most valuable of sales resources; they must be applied where they will have the highest probability of success. Even the fact that an individual can conceivably use a product is not always a legitimate reason to try to sell it. It is the ultimate satisfaction of both customer and company through proper placement of the product that is the goal.

An example: Once, in a chance conversation with a dignified, elderly country physician, I was asked what use a computer might serve in his practice. I discussed the fact that bills could be sent and accounting information maintained that would give him the precise amount of money owed by each patient. The physician was somewhat interested in this capability, but I pointed out that a computer could only provide information concerning delinquent debts; the collection of these debts would be up to the physician and his staff. Knowing that this individual was rapidly approaching retirement age and was not in need financially, I asked him, "If we were able to give you a computer report each month to show precisely who owed you money and how much, would you make a really serious effort to collect? His answer was as I suspected. "Probably not," he replied. "Then providing you with information you would not use might not be helpful and might even frustrate you," I said. "You might not benefit from computer processing of your accounts receivable."

Our object is not to sell everyone; it is to sell the right ones. These are people who will be the kind of satisfied customer who will gain the fullest use from our product and be delighted with it. Attempts to sell friends, relatives, business associates, and others who might buy only because of a personal relationship with the salesperson and not a need for the product itself is wrong. The question must always be: Does this person have the ultimate potential to be a delighted customer based on the product's answering a genuine need? (The objective is customer delight – Deming.)

An individual selected from the list of names who has probable real need is moved in the process from the *names* stage to the *suspects* stage. The salesperson applies empathy and judgment to make this transition. The time spent in making the consideration should be short. The mental attitude of the salesperson should be neutral; he or she should view a name lacking a need as sales time saved that might have been wasted. In some ways, the identity of the best suspects will be intuitively obvious to the salesperson. Do not try to create suspects out of poor raw material. There are more productive things to do, such as converting real suspects to prospects.

Suspects

Suspects are those individuals or businesses who, from their observable characteristics, appear to have a high probability of having a real need for the product. The transition from being a name to being a suspect is made with little effort and energy on the part of the salesperson – just a quick look, a brief thought, then the name is on or off the suspect list.

Suspects merit some brief personal contact by the salesperson. They are individuals or businesses that appear to have potential need that fits the product's use. The purpose of the sales contact is to determine if a use for the product truly exists and, if so, whether the individual or business can be classed as a prospect. Using our foregoing example, we might have determined that Ajax Moving and Storage, Inc. is a suspect for a truck sale. We resolve to commit some added effort in making personal contact with Ajax to evaluate the opportunity.

Sales contact can be made in a number of ways, depending on the product, on the suspect, and on the number of suspects for that product. The challenge is to perform the most effective evaluation possible of the customer's need – or lack thereof – in the shortest possible time. At the same time, the evaluation must be thorough and appropriate enough to accurately determine need. Three common methods of contacting suspects are telephone, mail, and personal visits.

Regardless of the type of contact at this stage, the objective is to derive prospects from the group of suspects. Prospects are identified through the *qualification* process.

Qualification. The process of qualification is applied to a suspect to determine if he or she is or can be made a prospect. Much time and energy is wasted, particularly by novice sales personnel, in attempting to sell to businesses or individuals who could not have bought in the first place. This is a stage for real objectivity. To become a prospect, a suspect must, after the sales contact, be found to have the required:

- Need (real and agreed to);
- Desire (willingness to make a change);
- Money (sufficient to pay); and
- Authority (level sufficient to make the decision).

Three of these are rational components and one, desire, is an emotional one. Of the four listed requirements, only desire can be created. Almost implicit in desire, but worthy of emphasis, is the requirement that the individual or business indicate that the time frame for decision is sufficiently short to warrant an intense or immediate sales effort. As the decision-making time frame stretches out, complicating factors can always impinge on it.

Individuals within suspect businesses who lack the authority to make a buying decision may refer the salesperson to the appropriate higher level individual; they may also agree to make the introduction. This lower echelon contact might also communicate something of the business situation that could be of use in determining the direct applicability of the product.

Professional salespeople must concentrate effort on the

authentic potential customers – qualified prospects. When time and energy are wasted because of lack of qualification, salespeople can become demoralized when no one buys. They have, in truth, missed opportunities due to misdirected effort. Legitimate opportunities were not pursued because time was wasted on the unqualified. However it is expressed, the message is the same, and it cannot be overemphasized: expend effort only on those who can and want to buy – those who are qualified. One outstanding salesperson put it this way: "You have to separate the buyers from the tire kickers." Another quipped: "Never try to teach a pig to sing. It wastes your time and annoys the pig." Customers are not meant any disrespect by these expressions, but the somewhat colorful slang makes the message easier to remember.

No amount of sincere hope will make true what is not so. In the evaluation of suspects for reclassification as prospects, there is no room for sincere hope. A perfect example of the trouble and waste caused by believing that sincerity makes a difference in a situation dominated by reality was given in the installment of Charles Schulz's cartoon strip "Peanuts" in which Linus misses Halloween trick-or-treating with the other children while he waits faithfully in a pumpkin patch for the Great Pumpkin to come and bring toys to those children who believe in Him. Why does Linus think He will come? Because he waits in the "sincerest" pumpkin patch in the whole world!

Linus wastes Halloween, and numerous salespeople waste time and career because they don't approach qualification quickly and pragmatically. A friendly reception and pleasant conversation with a suspect lacking a qualification ingredient will not make them qualified. Such suspects, knowing they cannot buy, may become more conversational and friendly, but this is often from their guilt in wasting the salesperson's time. Salespeople must always be friendly and responsive, but they are not simply a visitation committee from their company; they represent solutions searching for problems. Professional salespeople should always be direction oriented. They don't waste their time or that of other people. If the product doesn't match the suspect's needs, they should bow out gracefully. Credibility is gained through saying the obvious: "We can't help you." This suspect may become a prospect at a later date. One must do what can reliably be done, but no more.

Contact Methodologies. We mentioned earlier that suspects may be contacted via mail, telephone, or a personal visit. There are other ways in which suspects may be solicited to respond, such as media ads. Since we are dealing chiefly with methods that offer a more personal approach, we will look at these only briefly.

Mail has the least personal touch in terms of interactivity and empathy. The rejection rate is high, with only a maximum of about 2 percent of the usual mailings to suspects generating a response. Much depends on the message conveyed concerning product use and value. The chief advantage of mail is that it is relatively inexpensive and uses little of the salesperson's time in relation to the number of persons contacted. The purpose of most mailings is simply to determine existing interest in, and need for, the product. A positive response to a mailing can be followed up by a telephone call or a personal visit. Where possible and appropriate, a telephone call can be most effective while requiring little time.

Many texts and courses are offered that deal specifically with the telephone and its use in selling. Students should consult these for an in-depth review of telephone techniques. The following observation may add to the understanding and usefulness of the telephone in selling situations.

Properly used, the telephone can be the most efficient and effective of selling tools. To realize its potential, the individual salesperson must sound confident and comfortable using it. Telephone "prospecting" is an individual preference, but its benefits make it worth the effort to acquire proficiency.

Many executives today have their calls screened by a secretary or by answering systems because they do not wish to waste time on useless calls. An air of confidence and competence must be evident in one's phone calls to ensure that the call does not sound useless and that it overcomes such barriers. It is often appropriate to chat briefly with the secretary, sometimes inquiring as to who in the organization would be the appropriate individual to contact concerning the product. The mode should be friendly and conversational. A clear introduction, along with the company name, should accompany a request for help and guidance. Most people respond positively to a friendly voice and a request for help; both are threat reducers. Your voice should sound natural and comfortable, not canned or stiff. It is difficult to describe, but a telephone voice can be developed that sounds as though it is used to being listened to and not used to being ignored. It doesn't have to have the tenor of Henry Kissinger's voice, but that's the idea.

The desired result is to be permitted a brief contact with the decision maker to quickly determine or identify a specific interest or need for the product. Be prepared to be cut short sometimes, but also be prepared to find that by being pleasant and to the point you will be afforded a few minutes of contact. Ask your suspect if this is an appropriate time for him or her to talk briefly. If the answer is yes, then attention has been committed; if not, ask when might be a more convenient time to call back. Either way, the salesperson usually buys a few minutes. Use the phone to determine need and interest and to set up a personal visit or other suitable follow-up.

The company's name and its reputation can have a strong initial impact, but it buys only the first 10 or 15 seconds; personal credibility must take over from that point. A common event for almost everyone these days is to be called at home in the evening by someone attempting to sell something, but a business call should be placed to the office of a suspect for professional selling unless the customer specifically asks to be called at home.

Entrées, or references provided by other customers, also gain telephone advantage. Many people will listen for a few minutes to salespeople referred by a trusted colleague or friend. This can afford the salesperson peer status and consideration as a product source. Use the time given professionally: get right to the point, determine a specific need or interest, set a follow-up visit to explore further, and then gracefully break off the conversation.

Building Qualification with Suspects. Our earlier discussion of qualification characteristics was not at all meant to imply that salespeople must look only for suspects who are in a "ready" state – that is, who already meet all the requirements of qualification. There is always the possibility to move a suspect to qualified prospect status through effective selling.

The point to keep in mind is that the objective is efficiency in selling – gaining positive results in the least time. Efficiency requires prioritizing sales efforts to put the most effort on the opportunities with the best probable return. In qualifying prospects it is sometimes useful to categorize the salesperson's entire list of sales opportunities in order to get a clearer picture of where opportunities lie so that sales attention may be most profitably directed. Every professional salesperson prioritizes activities according to a mental picture of opportunity, but organizing them in chart format offers great advantages. This method offers insights for both salespeople and for their company into what their "ideal" customer profile is and what factors might be added to strengthen sales performance.

Suspect Contact Record. No sales contact is truly a waste of time. To find that a suspect is not really qualified saves both his or her time and the salesperson's. The most productive sales efforts will be those directed at qualified prospects. However, there will be times in which no "qualified" prospects are in view and a question arises about what might be done to find or develop some. The answer lies in maintaining simple but useful records on the results of suspect contacts. A suspect ranking based on the number of qualifying criteria that were present becomes the key to efficiency. In practice, it might work this way:

> Marsha Jones is a sales representative for a national life insurance firm. As the month of February came to a close, Marsha discovered that she had closed all the qualified prospects she had and was forced to admit that she didn't know where the next sale might arise. Marsha, however, had made it a practice to keep a simple set of records in her laptop

computer. Each time she made a contact, she completed a record and entered it into her contact file. The record contained the name, title, address, phone number, and date of each contact, along with a short, one-line comment section. The heart of the record, however, was three little boxes labeled as follows:

- Needs it
- Knows it
- Decision

With each sales contact, Marsha had entered an "X" in each of the boxes that applied to that particular suspect. The few seconds in creating a simple call record database was about to pay off. As the computer read through the over 152 records in the box, it sorted the records into groups based on the total number of "X" marks for each suspect. Of course, none of these suspect cards contained more than two "X" marks; otherwise, they would have been qualified and rated prospects. Forty-eight records had at least two "X" marks. Marsha then paged through and eliminated the records that did not have an "X" mark in the "Needs it" box. That left 16 records with an indication that the suspect needed insurance but lacked only one of the other factors.

Marsha read the first record: Carol Wilson. Comment: Expecting baby – husband not home. The contact date was October of the previous year. Now Marsha remembered: Carol's husband was out of town on a business trip on the original contact. Carol agreed that she needed insurance, but she had some with the company with which she was employed. Carol was thinking of leaving her job when the baby came and her husband wasn't home to discuss their situation. Carol could make a decision herself, but it was the decision box that Marsha had not checked; Carol hadn't known their time frame for considering insurance. At the time of the contact, it was certainly months away.

Marsha picked up the phone and called Carol. The baby had arrived, was doing fine, and yes, she had left her job. Things had changed and now might be appropriate to consider adding life insurance, not only to cover Carol, but for the baby as well. Marsha scheduled a visit for that evening with Carol and her husband.

The message for salespeople is that just as work has been expended and expense incurred in producing in-process inventory in a manufacturing situation, so sales effort and contact costs money and time. The result of that effort is information that has value. Things change, even for suspects. Yesterday's suspect may be tomorrow's prospect. The converse is also true; that is why diligent and intense effort must be applied to close business with prospects when they are qualified and in decision mode.

Using Marsha's three-point rating system, a suspect who needs a product, knows or agrees that it is needed, but is not ready to consider a decision in the near future would be classed as an "A" suspect. Those who, in the estimation of the salesperson, truly need the product but are not convinced themselves would be called "B" suspects. Those who everyone, including the salesperson, agree have no need for the product are called "C" suspects and should not be contacted in the future unless some change occurs with either the product or themselves.

A most important point to remember in consideration of moving B suspects into the A category and elevating A suspects to Prospect status is that this is not an easy effort. Efficiency in selling demands that energy be spent addressing opportunities based on a priority of potential return. Moving suspects into higher levels and eventually to prospect status requires serious effort. The more ingredients present in the beginning, the better. The hierarchy based on sales potential just discussed keeps the sales focus where it belongs – on legitimate opportunity.

A *suspect* plus *qualification* yields a *prospect*.

Prospects

This is where the professional salespeople of the Quality Era must focus their time and energy, because a truly qualified Prospect is worth it. These individuals:

- Need a solution your product can offer;
- Can take action quickly if they can be shown that the product meets their need;

- Have the financial resources to buy, and
- Have the authority to make the decision.

In most professional selling situations, there are usually only a few individuals in view at any one time who are truly qualified prospects. These can be identified after the sifting and refining effort made in the two previous stages. They are people who are ready to buy. The product represents an answer to their need, but competitive products may also be under consideration. The prospect can feel that a certain type of product is the answer but is undecided about the best source. The issue has now evolved to one of "which" and is no longer "whether."

At this point, the salesperson must begin working with the prospect to develop the comprehensive solution that he or she will ultimately be expected to buy. The development of a buying decision, as outlined in Chapter 5, is the approach that allows the business to be earned by developing a comprehensive and complete sale, one that bonds the customer to the salesperson and ultimately to the parent company. Because this process is so essential, the entire previous chapter was dedicated to a review of the buying decision.

In development of the buying decision, certain overall points should be kept in perspective by the salesperson. The prospect should be seen as the individual with the problem, and the salesperson should view himself or herself as the one with the solution. The salesperson should maintain a consultant stance and attitude and be ready to help the customer to outline complete conceptual expectations and clear needs for a solution and to listen and question empathetically. This is somewhat equivalent to the tone taken by a personal physician conducting a physical exam or an architect determining what kind of home his client desires. The salesperson has seen the needs the product has fulfilled for others and can suggest and list problems with the current situation and the benefits and advantages that should result from the purchase of the product. Prospects respond most positively to genuine understanding of their problem and feelings. The salesperson should restate these problems and frustrations just as the prospect has related them to ensure that both parties clearly understand the need.

Upon complete understanding of the problem – *and only then* – should the salesperson begin discussing in general terms a product concept that might meet the customer's needs. There should be a mutual building of a solution based on retaining any positive aspects of the current approach that the prospect feels are advantageous and the replacement of any objectionable or deficient characteristics by the new product approach. This structuring of a solution concept that conserves the positive and eliminates the negative is basic to motivation. The salesperson will establish two mental pictures in the mind of the prospect: one of the old approach with its problems and frustrations, and one of the new approach based on added benefits and advantages of the proposed product. The imaginatively developed image of the new approach must appeal to the prospect to an extent that it causes heightened interest and an intensified desire sufficient to buy the new and reject the old. Reminding the prospect of the positive characteristics that will remain unchanged increases comfort and confidence in the new approach. The salesperson must *never* begin a discussion of the product (i.e., the specific solution) until the prospect's need is fully understood and confirmed.

Competition

Sales competitors will attempt to do a similar thing with their products. The decision to buy will be made in the mind of the customer. The salesperson who is perceived to best understand the prospect's problem will most often be entrusted with the solution. As the true needs of the prospect are discussed, it should become clear to both salesperson and prospect that no two products are precisely the same in total design approach and function. The question is not which of the competitors offers the best solution; it might rather be stated that people are in the market for different things. The salesperson must help the prospect discover the relevant and significant points of positive differentiation to demonstrate that he or she is in the market for the salesperson's product, approach, or concept – and, therefore, that the salesperson's product represents the most appropriate solution. The following is an early illustration of this principle.

> According to the Biblical narrative, a pharaoh of Egypt had a dream that troubled him greatly. In the dream he saw seven fat cattle come up from the River Nile. These were followed by seven emaciated cattle, which ate up the fat cattle but were left just as lean as before. The scene then changed to seven ears of grain that were in wonderful condition, which were consumed by seven poor ears of grain. In those days, dreams were taken seriously, and to this king the similarity of the two visions reinforced their importance. But what to do? What did the visions mean?
>
> The king called his counselors and asked the meaning of the dream. None could tell it. But one had encountered a slave during a recent stay in prison who was able to interpret dreams. The pharaoh sent for this individual, who came, heard the story, and essentially said:
>
> "I understand why you are troubled by the dream. You should be. You are being given a chance to fix a major impending problem. Egypt is about to have seven years of agricultural plenty followed by seven years of such severe famine that the nation will be devastated."
>
> By this time Joseph, the slave, had the pharaoh's undivided attention, and his credibility was increasing. "What you need to do," continued Joseph, "is appoint a capable individual to store up the food in the plentiful years and dole it out in the lean years, and in this way you will keep everyone from starving and save Egypt."
>
> The pharaoh was impressed! Who is better to take on this assignment than Joseph (the guy who best understood the problem). Everyone agreed, and Joseph was promoted on the spot from slave to vice-pharaoh in charge of the whole project.[1]

The prospect's perception that the salesperson empathetically understands the problem earns confidence in his or her recommended solution, which also often means that the prospect not only buys the product but in a sense chooses the salesperson perceived to be best qualified to take charge of the implementation of the solution. This gives rise to the old adage that to sell a product one must first sell him or herself.

If the fit between product and customer is not proper and cannot be made so, the professional salesperson should state the obvious: "I do not have an answer that fits your needs." This maintains the salesperson's credibility and the respect of the prospect. There may be a product in the future that will meet those needs. Quality-oriented salespeople will guard their reputation at all costs; it is their most valuable possession. Frankness and honesty in sales discussions are essential in Quality Era selling. Salespeople must never appear to need the business. Appearing to need a sale can bring credibility into question. Desperation must never show. As another old adage states, "If there are holes in the soles of your shoes, then keep them flat on the floor."

Enjoy Selling

Dare to have fun. Remember Deming's call to find joy in your work. Uncovering prospect needs with the sure knowledge that your company's products can fix them is exciting. It is the stuff of which heroic stories are made. Obvious enjoyment of the sales discussion and interest in finding a solution will enliven the salesperson's personality and ensure a normal and comfortable discussion impossible with excessive strategizing and rigid regurgitation of memorized product facts. People buy from people they like; therefore, salespeople should be genuinely likeable. The object is to build a relationship, not just sell a product. This relationship is strengthened by both parties liking and trusting each other.[2]

Having done a credible job in developing a solution using the buying decision structure, the prospect should buy and thus become a new customer. When as a marketing manager I talked with new salespeople who had just made a sale and were feeling the excitement of being entrusted with a customer's commitment, I often facetiously asked why they seemed surprised. Their business card said "sales"; they should have been more surprised had they not sold something. The job is to sell; it should not come as a surprise.

Prospects Plus the Buying Decision = New Customer

A salesperson sells dreams but must deliver reality. The two should be compatible. Unmet expectations are the source of all customer dissatisfaction![3] A persuasive sales argument and word pictures that elicit positive visualizations are powerful agents; they must be used morally. The benefits projected imaginatively must be realized when the product is put into use. The objective of the salesperson should be to answer the customer's needs so well that more is delivered than was expected. The result is a delighted customer. (The objective is a delighted customer – Deming.)

Not only should the product perform, but the customer should see that the salesperson's interest in maintaining satisfaction is not diminished after the sale is made or an order signed. Personal commitment, not contracts, is the cement of Quality Era selling. Contracts and legal documents are the rigid boundaries of responsibility; they are not the foundation of a relationship. Contracts are fall-back legal measures to be used only if all else fails. Relationships are built on a spirit of engagement and partnership.

Conversely, relationships cannot be built on unrealistic demands by either party; sometimes customers and prospects need to be reasoned with to show why their demands or expectations lie outside the bounds of realistic performance. Customer respect is earned by the logical explanation of real performance limits. Setting proper expectations prior to accepting the order is key to avoiding these problems.

New customers are almost always insecure, cautiously expectant, and sensitized. They have committed; will the product's performance be up to their expectations? Customers often have these postsale concerns. They should see no reduction in the concern and attitude of the salesperson after receiving the order. This is for two reasons. The first is that the salesperson should still be focused on relationship, not the order; this perspective must always be kept in view. The second reason is sensitization.

Sensitization means that the new customer feels vulnerable and will take any perceived diminution of care and concern on the vendor's part as an indication that he or she may have made a mistake in the buying decision. Once the relationship has become longstanding, there is more understanding and give and take, but the initial stages of a customer relationship require special care. Vendor companies and salespeople should pay particular attention at this point. An unexpected call or letter from the salesperson or sales management can reassure the customer. Most important of all in building a relationship is that the quality of the customer support demonstrated is consistent with the preconceptions created during the initial selling process. Go overboard to make new customers feel appreciated and special. Surprise them with creative evidences of care and concern for their satisfaction.

As a marketing manager with IBM, I often would send a cake and large urn of coffee out to an installing computer account. Their people and our people had usually been working late hours with the installation of equipment. This little gesture, which just happened to arrive at an appropriate time when the salesperson dropped by, was always received positively. In many cases, company executives participated in these coffee breaks; in one case, a company president commented that this was one of the nicest things any vendor had ever done for his company. Do occasional unexpected things to show that you care for customers, not just their money. Art is not limited to paint and brushes.

A differentiation of the Quality Era company from other vendors should become increasingly more visible to new customers. Conduct relationships with them on a high plane and with professionalism. Doing just a little bit more than is expected and with a little bit more quality and caring separates one from the herd. Great things can be done on a small budget; the key is caring, creativity, and empathy. Quality in relationship building is stimulating, but one must really care. This empathy must be consistent. No business has a department of caring; it must be shown by all departments and individuals. Caring will be the pervasive spirit of the successful Quality Era company – an attitude that will be communicated through all products and

135

service with originality and consistency. It can add flavor to life. Customers respond. Employees respond. New dimensions open.

New Customer Plus Service and Support = Delighted Customer

There are customers who have been patrons of the vendor company for some time. A mutual familiarity now exists, but there should be no diminishment in service or caring. Every customer needs to be seen as important – and to be made to *feel* important – to the vendor company. Informative channels between customer management and vendor management should be opened and maintained above the normal sales contact. Any hint of product dissatisfaction must be addressed. This does not mean that every customer's whim needs to be gratified. Customers understand that problems arise and will most often work with the vendor toward a mutually acceptable solution. It is a perceived lack of caring and attention on the part of salespeople that fractures relationships.

The ability and willingness of an organization to do unusual things to address a customer problem accomplishes much more than a problem fix; little and big heroics accomplished in doing the remarkable build company legends. These legends form the company culture; they build pride in the organization and interdepartmental respect. These legends differentiate the Quality Era company both to itself and its customers, and they become part of the company's identity. *Every customer problem has inherent within it the opportunity to demonstrate the positive actions the vendor company is capable of performing.* It is in these situations that legends and war stories about exceptional response and customer service are born. These are told over and over again by employees and customers. In a recent presentation, a noted business leader commented that it is possible to measure the morale of a business by the stories its employees tell about their company. Are the heroic stories told of events long past, or is the company generating new stories? This can tell a great deal about the quality tone of the company. A Quality Era company that is not generating new stories of brilliant handling of customer requirements is in trouble.

When customer relationship is strengthened over time, it becomes hard to break. Loyal customers will notify a traditional source vendor of attempted competitive approaches and allow it to respond. They can also creatively critique the vendor service and product offerings, thereby assisting the vendor's design and development groups. Subsequent sales to established customers should be made more efficiently than the first sale. Procedures are understood, personnel are acquainted, and the familiar product design and service approach has become the standard by which competitive vendors and products are measured.

The established customer group can also often be involved with the design of new products and procedures with the sales group performing the introductions. Customer personnel will often make themselves available to consult with vendor design engineers and other departments that are searching for new approaches to product and service offerings. Many vendor organizations have created customer advisory boards to facilitate customer communications. In all such approaches, the customer's time must be respected and the results of such advice be apparent. Improved customer service is of value not just to the vendor but to the customer as well.

Customers Plus Partnership = Selling Customers

The ultimate objective of the sales continuum is to establish selling customers – that is, customers who proselytize to others about the quality of the vendor and its products. These companies or individuals can even serve as demonstration sites to confirm a product's functionality and quality. Everyone expects salespeople to be positive about their products, but a delighted user who tells others about a product is the most credible and effective of sales allies. The objective of the sales continuum is to bring as many customers as possible to this status, thus creating an effective auxiliary sales team.

Because customer, prospect, and sales information flowing to the operations and development divisions within a vendor company must become a continuous process, what we have called the sales continuum becomes a cycle rather than a straight line. In effect, businesses of the future will increasingly couple their design and manufacturing expertise with customer input to build products that the customers will want to buy in the future. Customers will even feel partial ownership of products they had a hand in developing. The patterns of bonding and the integration of customer's and vendor's businesses that are becoming evident today will continue. In the future it will become more difficult to determine where the vendor stops and customer starts. The linkage and joint planning fostered by the sales group will continue to grow and build the business partnership structures of the Quality Era.

Summary

The sales continuum is a structured process view of the methodology by which an individual or business moves from being an unknown entity to enthusiastic, familiar customer. By viewing this process and its stages as a continuum, numerical objectives can be set for team or individual performance at each stage of the continuum, which is subject to continuous quality improvement based on the refinement of technique and the measurement of results.

This flow lends itself well to the use by management of a simple database technology from which any and all individuals within the vendor business should be able to view the individual or business opportunity queued up at each stage of the process by the sales group. This is, of course, dependent upon the sales organization entering timely and accurate information and actually making full use of the system. The information system of a business is similar to a dollhouse version of a real house. If furniture is moved in the real house, the equivalent piece must be moved in the dollhouse or the dollhouse model is no longer true to the original – the model does not represent the real situation. As the continuum is installed and used properly, management and the sales group can both benefit.

Dr. Deming strongly believed that systems and circumstances presently govern the production levels of most individual workers. For a company to improve its workers' productivity, he believed, management must change the system and eliminate or de-emphasize performance measurement based solely on results. As the sales continuum is established as a process structure, aspects of sales performance that can actually be controlled by the salesperson can be viewed and measured as part of performance. For instance, a salesperson may not have made a sale in a week. This may have been due purely to circumstance. He or she can, however, control some aspects of the sales continuum situation by contacting 50 suspects to develop prospects. If the process he or she is following is quality capable and they follow it properly, results will in fact follow.

In the Quality Era, it is incumbent on management to establish systems or processes that are capable of producing quality results and to expect employees, including those in the sales group, to faithfully execute their stages of the process. Thus structure is provided for putting continuous quality improvement theory into action.

Notes

1. Exodus 41:1– 44.
2. Adam Smith makes this observation about being likable and showing interest and enthusiasm: "Nothing is more graceful than habitual cheerfulness, which is always founded upon a particular relish for all the little pleasures which common occurrences afford. We readily sympathize with it; it inspires us with the same joy, and makes every trifle turn up to us in the same agreeable aspect in which it represents itself to the person endowed with this happy disposition." [*Moral Sentiments*, p. 99]
3. Thus far, the term "customer" has often been used to mean the individual who is the target of a salesperson's efforts. In this section, a "customer" is an individual who has actually made a purchase.

CHAPTER 7

MEASUREMENTS FOR QUALITY SELLING

Profound concepts are often phrased in shirtsleeve terms. One of these is attributed to the inventor and manufacturer of the Klipsch horn, one of the finest high-fidelity loudspeakers ever developed. This gentleman once observed that "You can't build what you can't measure, because you won't know when you've got it made."

Any process must have an ultimate goal and have measurement characteristics that will indicate how close or how far from the goal one is at any time. Equally important is being able to know when the quest is complete so a new goal can be set. In a business organization, goals must be simple enough to be understood by all employees. They must also include visible components that make the progress toward success evident to all.

In the Quality Era, definite performance standards for processes must be established to secure a dependable level of performance and to ensure that erratic deviations from desired range do not occur. Unless a business activity or process is first brought to a consistent level of basic performance, efforts at quality improvements are futile and misplaced.[1]

For example, suppose that a company has determined that one range of quality customer service that it will offer will be that its phone will always be answered within four rings. Staffing and equipment will be provided to support this "process" within these limits. The first issue in quality development is to ensure that this performance range defines the process limits at all times and without exception. Only when the phone is being answered reliably within four rings can one effectively begin work toward an even better response such as three rings or improving the employees' conversational telephone technique or their response to customer service issues.

One of Deming's key concepts is that quality improvement

can only begin when systems have been put in place that control variation within dependable limits. Until a dependable performance range is attained with a system, the quality potential of that system itself cannot be known or improved. Thus, there are really two phases in quality improvement. The first is to eliminate extraneous variation. If the process is then shown to have difficulty performing reliably within acceptable limits, the process itself will need to be rethought and redesigned to create a process capable of performing within desired limits. Second, once a process is established that delivers consistently within desired limits, then efforts can be continually applied to reduce normal variations within the process and improve the results still further toward a single optimum performance standard. Thus the outer limits of the bell curve of performance are gradually pulled in toward the center and variation from the mean eliminated.

The focus of this chapter is to discuss individual process stages within the sales continuum and to suggest methodology for setting baseline performance standards for each. Once these functions are being performed reliably by the sales organization, efforts can be directed at continuously improving the actual quality of each process.

An instance that illustrates just how ludicrous the quest for quality can appear when this is not understood and approached properly involves a situation in which a customer made repeated calls to a sales office without getting an answer. On the third attempt, the phone was answered by a very frustrated temporary employee, who stated, "It has been very hectic around here today; I'm sorry you didn't get through, but all our regular people have been in a big *quality* meeting." One may not be able *always* to answer the phone within four rings, but letting it ring more than four times, if that is the initial quality limit, should be a very rare exception. One must not rush into refinements of quality until dependable process basics are in place.

Quality is the icing on the cake, not the cake itself. Customers are beginning to expect good cakes with good icing and candles as well. A business often needs to go back to basics and review its recipe and the cake-making process. This must be done pragmatically, for, as someone once said, "wherever you find yourself, there you are."

The first step toward improvement of quality is an honest assessment of where the business is at that moment. Management should view the business through the customer's eyes, gain information firsthand, and test the validity of that information by checking other sources. Managers will be surprised to find that the customer "hotline" is not "hot" or that "standard" procedures are not at all "standard." A sincere belief that everything is and will be all right is hazardous to quality improvement. Systems and processes are either working consistently or not. There will be no gain without facing reality.

Comprehensive Measurements

Only *proper* measurements can reveal the essential truths about present performance. Measurements for quality must not be set up lightly. Studies have indicated that some business executives who manage by "gut feel" or instinct sometimes do as well as those who rely totally on statistical methodologies. Quality Era management, as outlined by Deming, incorporates statistics as well as personal insight based on quality philosophy. Remember, he emphasized that one third of the good comes from statistics and two thirds comes from how we deal with people. The effective synergy of statistical measures and interpersonal undestanding can produce leadership. Deming felt that American business has had too much numerical management and too little leadership. The successful sales manager of today will be the one who is astutely gauging both the statistical and the human aspects and acting or reacting appropriately.

Statistics are not needed to affirm the obvious. Management observation must take place where the employees and customers are. If an inventory report says that there is a plentiful stock of an item but customers are shouting that they can't get it, the customer is the one to believe. There is a problem somewhere, and customer satisfaction is the measurement point to watch. It is strange to see it raining torrents outside and hear the radio state that there is a 70-percent probability of rain. Statistics are of great value in dealing with complex issues but sometimes are poor in answering specific concerns. If one customer walks away dissatisfied, that dissatisfaction can only be measured as being 100 percent. Statistical data in regard to buying decisions are made up of individual binary decisions, each 100 percent yes or 100 percent no. Focus on each of the individual decisions and the broader statistics will ultimately be favorable.

Misdirected Measurements

For a few years, I worked as a sales representative for a large pharmaceutical firm that manufactured a complete line of medicines marketed directly to physicians. As a measurement, each representative reported daily on the sales calls made and on the products presented. Since pharmacy orders for the company's products sold through drug wholesalers could be tracked, these were correlated with sales calls to determine the effectiveness of the salespeople. Right?

Well, maybe. If in the course of sales calls the salesperson found that colds and flu were reaching epidemic proportions in the territory, he or she would promote heavily those medicinal agents related to treating colds and flu. As a natural consequence of the epidemic, everyone's sales, including competition's, would be up; when the impact of effective selling was added, sales success was assured. Sales volumes were obviously correlating with promotional activity, which was what the company wanted. What was actually being measured here was the level of colds and flu.

Management should never be surprised to find measurements in place that make it easier for a department's or function's performance to appear positive while discovering at the same time that the function being so measured has little real relation to the desired overall business performance. The smug satisfaction of a department that is meeting its goals can prove a barrier to recognizing need for change and making quality improvements.

Narrow Departmental Measurements

I recently heard a presentation by the vice president of quality for one of America's premier food manufacturing companies that dealt with his experience in reviewing customer satisfaction criteria and divisional performance. During such a review, it became obvious to him that one of his company's divisions was demonstrating outstanding performance with customer deliveries in comparison with other groups, and he made arrangements to visit them in order to present them with an award for their excellent performance. During this visit, the vice president discovered that this division was measuring the time from order receipt to the time the order left *their* shipping dock; the other divisions were factoring in actual transit time to measure how long it took for the merchandise to actually arrive at the *customer's* dock.

If measurements do not measure what should be measured, management may be handing out awards for creative measurement structuring rather than for customer-related performance. Since incentive produces behavior, employees may even become very adept at creating and meeting irrelevant measurement criteria. They may even be promoted and carry this expertise to management levels.

Only involved top management can overview the business and ensure the implementation of proper measurements – those that focus on customer satisfaction and business efficiency. If a measurement structure doesn't translate into improved customer service or companywide efficiency, it is at the least irrelevant and may actually be counterproductive. The sales force can be as guilty of this as any other group or department.

An example of measurement in isolation occurred in a major computer firm, which had prepared and distributed an excellent brochure. It included a short, pertinent questionnaire about sales that prospects were asked to complete and send back to the computer company, which would analyze this data and then follow up with a visit by a sales representative.

After some months, no response was observed by the sales group. In an effort to check the effectiveness of this marketing approach, a call was made to the marketing communications department that had been assigned the task of handling customer responses to the questionnaire. This group replied that the response had been excellent – over 150 customer questionnaires were completed and returned. The question was then asked: "How many of the leads have resulted in customer sales?" "We don't know the answer to that," they replied.

Further discussion revealed that the marketing communications department had simply counted the completed responses, placed them on file, and had not forwarded the responses to the appropriate field sales representatives. Their departmental measurement of the brochure's success was simply based on the number of prospect responses generated by a promotional campaign, which they had faithfully logged before pronouncing this program successful. Nothing else had been done. As a manager, it is not safe to assume that anything is happening automatically or correctly. As one management realist expressed, "You get what you inspect, not what you expect." Quality in selling is derived from reaching the people who count, rather than counting the people you reach.

Process Measurement

Since customers do things for their own reasons, much of the selling process and therefore the sales continuum are not amenable to precise numerical measurement of predictive accuracy. In fact it can seem much of selling falls under the newer concepts of chaos which relate that variables that are impossible to measure precisely cause system results to vary beyond predictability.[2] Deming agreed that "the most important numbers relating to the management of a business may be unknown and indeed unknowable.[3]" If so much is random, then how can structure and measurement be usefully applied? The answer lies in understanding the power of process structure and the concept it enables called continuous process improvement. Just as the concepts of the assembly line and interchangeable parts (both process concepts) enabled dramatic advances in industrial production the injection of process concepts into the sales process can produce enormous benefit.

Those aspects of the sales process which can be structured and performed under process methodology can and should be so structured. Those aspects of a subjective nature which are not so amenable must be left to the skill and judgement of salespeople and management. What is established melds art and science to enable progress toward quality.

The sales continuum view of selling as a process is powerful because it establishes a framework of processes that relate to each other and contribute to the overall objective of producing sales results. In the past too much emphasis has been placed on individual sales results and not on the process as a whole. In fact good results can make management believe that they have a process that must be working. The quality era is calling management to pay less attention to the immediate results and more to the quality capabilities of processes and their execution. It can prove most difficult for management and sales personnel historically focused on results to switch to an equal emphasis on process, but that is precisely what must occur. It is essential to understand that it is the quality capabilities of the processes and their ingredients which ultimately produce lasting and continuously improving results. The Quality Era business is not in competition with its competitors' salespeople but ultimately with their own business processes.

A clear modern example of the power of this process approach is that of franchise business. McDonald's for instance, is based on a business concept thoroughly implemented through specific processes faithfully executed in identical fashion at every location. If the concept and its processes produce a perceived superior product for the customer the business grows and more franchises are opened doing the same thing the same way. Some superficial individuality may be evident but underneath at the process level they strictly adhere to uniform but continuously improving methodology. It is in the establishment of the processes which comprise the operation in which the resultant success of the operation rests. Management establishes and confirms a comprehensive set of processes, and employees execute these faithfully. The sales results depend on the process as much as on the individuals executing the process. This is not to say that individual capabilities do not powerfully supplement the process and add to its success. But the message is that process design and execution are essential. It is on processes and their improvement (with the willing participation of and innovative suggestions of employees) that management of the Quality Era will focus.

The Japanese concept of *Kaizen* (continuous quality improvement) is of great use in situations when quality improvement is desirable but specific measurements are not possible. The process view and structure allow the measurement of the consistency with which operations within the process are carried out. As the employee works consistently through the defined process, quality results will occur over time *because the process is capable of producing quality results.* Faithful execution of the process by employees and their suggestions and efforts to improve the process are considered as important as the intended result. [4]

Establishing procedural standards for consistency in the sales continuum can start at the point at which the customer's need is determined. As mentioned earlier, the sales group is the organization closest to the mind of the customer and therefore a natural source for identifying and confirming such needs. Ideas for products or services brought forward by the sales organization should be clearly defined and then presented for evaluation by all appropriate personnel. Ideas submitted by the sales group should be defined thoroughly in concept and, just as importantly, related from an empathetic standpoint. How are the customers reacting to the present product or its status? What will their reaction be to a new concept?

We wish not just to make new products, but to make new products that will sell because they meet unfolding customer needs. Innovations must be designed with customer attitudes as well as functional improvement in mind. These attitudes must be fully and clearly articulated, and once they are confirmed through surveys and the dialog between salesperson and customer, they should not be reinterpreted. Just as a message passed in whispers around a room by successive individuals will mutate, the basic customer intent with regard to product needs can be altered, which could result in the final product being far off the mark in terms of the concepts that gave rise to its development. A famous comic once remarked that for a thing to be humorous it must have a basis of truth. Figure 7.1 illustrates what can occur during product development if there is a lack of clear communications. The inclusion of detailed, verbatim customer need and attitudes reaffirm the design direction for innovation and ensure that the new concept is precisely on target.

Customer need should be defined and confirmed by:

- *Input from salespeople.* This can outline the customers' needs, attitudes, and perception of value.
- *Marketing surveys.* These can define and/or confirm the customers' needs and how they perceived the advantages offered by the product.
- *Customer reviews.* These can help us to see what the customer thinks of the product's design and function.
- *Sample testing.* This helps to determine the customers' preferences and to predict the acceptance level that the product will achieve.

All efforts should be designed to capture the "why" behind the customers' desire for innovation. It is most valuable to discover what if anything is wrong with the old approach or product so that these aspects can be eliminated and to determine what is right with the old approach so that these factors can be retained and even enhanced.

This should sound familiar. It is the buying decision at work in the design process. In this methodology, older products should be viewed as if they belonged to a competitor and the new item under evaluation should be seen as a potential new entry product for the vendor company. In an age of continual quality competition, businesses must be capable of continual modification so that today's model is always superior to yesterday's. The concept of continuous quality improvement injects the idea of product evaluation and modification on a continual basis rather than the old concept of a "yearly model" that incorporated all accumulated changes. Why not make next week's product better than this week's, and so on? Products must be designed to fit the customers' needs and desires, to eliminate their frustrations, and to delight them. If the production and sales approaches now

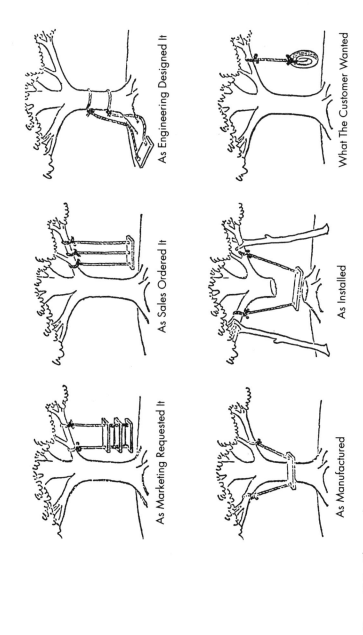

As Marketing Requested It

As Sales Ordered It

As Engineering Designed It

As Manufactured

As Installed

What The Customer Wanted

Figure 7.1. The product

149

in place do not allow for continual improvement, they need to be revamped or replaced with processes that do.[1]

As we have outlined, one of the quality measurements for selling in the sales continuum is the process of identifying individuals or businesses that are appropriate for further attention and/or progressive movement to the next stage. Advancement to each successive stage represents a decision based on objective measurements. Sales management must measure honestly how many opportunities are being produced at each stage of the sales continuum and thus document present standards of performance. As quality innovations are implemented, changes in output at each stage can be measured against the original values to gauge the effect of the changes. The crucial quality measurement criteria is thus the increase in the rate at which individuals are properly moved forward in the stages of the sales continuum. This can be measured when a process view is applied and a current level performance for each stage is established.

Designing Products to Sell

Properly designed products should have a written product plan which addresses each buying decision element, stated in the specific *customer* terms including:

- A clear statement of need(s) for the product.
- A definition by the customers of why they desire innovation in the product area – how they view the deficiencies of current products and the problem caused by these deficiencies.
- The justification of the product through the determination of a benefit-to-cost ratio that shows how the customer will value the features of the new product.
- A well-articulated design concept based on the customers' needs, desires, and justification as well as the ease of implementing the new product. (A rational, teachable, concept)
- A thorough, sensible plan of customer implementation confirmed acceptable by customers.

- The increased vendor credibility with the customers, who recognize that the previous decision points have been well-conceived, logical, and not been surrounded by hype.

As a measurement standard, all new products and changes under review should carry with their documentation a brief outline detailing precisely how the new item addresses each of the buying decision elements just discussed. Quality Era selling calls first for all products to be designed with the selling process (i.e., the buying decision and the sales contiuum) in mind.

The implementation of other key measurements can make a significant difference in sales performance. As emphasized earlier, all measurements need not be numerical or exact. Selling is an area of performance that deals with broad, subjective concepts. The consistent performance of a specific function is often the measured activity. Once reliable performance is established, improvements in the quality of each function become the task of subjective leadership by management.

Predesign Measurements – The Need for a New Item

Is there a verified need for a new feature or function directed by the customer? Here, "verified" means that the company has clearly defined what it understands to be the customer need and, just as importantly, has defined the customer reaction and feelings that have been produced because this need is unmet. When presented with a clearly written description of this need and these reactions, do a high percentage of customers confirm them? Do all involved departments within the business have the capability to restate the need and its consequences in the terms voiced by customers? Particularly, does the sales force at the field level agree in all points with the statement of need and the customer's anticipated reaction? If all of these criteria are met, product development may proceed. The present approach and the new approach can both be mapped on a situation dynamic chart. Figure 7.2 shows a situation dynamic chart for the Acme Model #1 can opener.

The chart is essentially a form of vector analysis. The pros

Existing Product: Acme Model #1 Can Opener	
Pro	**Con**
It opens cans reliably.	It is slow to use with multiple cans.
It is easy to use.	Manual usage - it tires its users.
It works on all can sizes.	It produces lids that are jagged, which can cut the user.
It is highly portable.	It is more expensive than some others.
It is relatively inexpensive.	
It almost never breaks.	
It is small, takes little space, and stores easily.	
Sales Equilibrium	

Note: The Relative Importance of Pro's and Con's should be indicated by ranking them from most important at the top to least important at the bottom.

Figure 7.2. An example of a situation dynamic chart.

and cons represent the driving and restraining forces perceived to interact in the marketplace to produce the equilibrium or status quo in sales performance of a product. If positive forces (pros) can be accentuated or added and negative forces (cons) reduced or eliminated, sales volumes should increase and a new equilibrium should be established.

In creating such a chart, each point (pro or con) should be stated as a complete, clear sentence to ensure a complete statement of the characteristic being described. These sentences should then be expanded into a statement of how customers view the feature as an advantage or a disadvantage. For example, a positive customer view of a product could take the form of a statement such as: "It opens cans reliably, so that customers remark that it has served them well for years. They wish that other appliances were as reliable." An example of a negative attitude would be a statement such as: "It produces a jagged edge on the lid, which is sharp and can cut a user. Thus, users must be careful and are apprehensive of lids and cans opened with it."

From these statements of pro and con features, a set of design criteria for a new or improved product can be developed that includes features and their impact on customer satisfaction.

The concept under consideration for implementation should be validated by customer contact when discretion can be maintained. A letter of nondisclosure can be used to reinforce the importance of confidentiality with customers and with internal personnel. The benefits of customer review and their assent to the new approach may be well worth the risk of competition's finding out about the planned innovation. Customers, of course, are individuals and there is no one "mind of the customer" per se, but there will be certain consistent themes of customer need that will be voiced again and again. It is these consistent themes that must be understood thoroughly. Some may want red widgets and some will want blue widgets, but they all want widgets.

Quality Lists and Quality Data

Sales organizations are penalized severely when they work from name and suspect lists that contain many errors. In terms of the selling process, such lists are analogous to poor raw material. It is not just the frustration of finding that the data provided do not check out in reality; there is also the attitudinal erosion toward the salesperson's company that can take place.

Management should provide its salespeople with quality lists and information for the same reason it gives its customers quality products: to increase confidence in – and thus commitment to – the company. The creation and maintenance of the information systems lists and data pertinent to the sales continuum as it is generated and maintained prevent a duplication of effort. It also ensures a continuity of coverage and the progress of the process despite personnel changes.

The maintenance of reliable customer status data will prevent a lost investment of sales effort. For this reason it is also highly desirable that salespeople be responsible for their own sales activity data as related to the sales continuum into the information system, but always according to format standards that permit this information to be summarized and processed as required by other departments and management at all levels within the company. The benefits of this approach can save both management and the sales organization vast amounts of time previously spent developing status reports, because the information is constantly available via the system.

Management should be able to take a comprehensive look at the sales picture and the overall sales continuum at any time without having to make specific requests for reports from the departments involved. For example, if information on all qualified prospects for each territory is routinely entered into each salesperson's personal sales information database along with all prospect sales potential, the percent probability of closing the sale and the estimated date of that closing, then management, by accessing the salesperson's individual system, can get a sales forecast *at any time* for each salesperson or for the entire sales group without interrupting sales activity to have reports produced.

The key, of course, is to have a well-structured database system and to have the sales personnel using it consistently in maintaining accurate data. The measurement criteria here must be accurate and complete data entered daily by the sales group so that individual or consolidated information drawn from this data will be accurate and timely. The information system must be used efficiently by the sales force in planning selling strategies. Management's reports are a valuable byproduct drawn automatically and without fanfare as needed.

Measuring the Sales Continuum as a Process

Sales management should set numerical targets for salespeople to reach at each point along the sales continuum and should monitor the continuum as a process with expected levels of production at each point. These goals can only be set by knowledgeable management using optimal performance as a guide to determine the quality standards for the sales group. For instance it may be determined that each day 30 new names will be evaluated to select at least 6 suspects to be called from which (on average) one prospect will be qualified. If currently the selling process is yielding a 50% close ratio of qualified prospects then this activity effectively executed will produce 2.5 sales each week. With improvement of the process over time the close rate will increase. The key is to understand and construct and execute the process through which "Names" become customers.

As new customers are managed effectively through the implementation and service processes they mature into delighted selling customers. These customers supply the vendor with a dependable stream of business, advise on product development, and assist in selling others. The sales continuum is now a completed cycle.

Nine measurement points that sales managers and salespeople should consider systematizing, monitoring, and continously improving are:

- Prospect qualifications
- Prospect handicapping system
- Proposal reviews
- Sales forecasts
- Buying decisions
- Customer satisfaction contacts
- Customer acceptance reviews
- Support systems response time
- Salesperson technique

Prospect Qualification Methodology

As we've already pointed out, before a suspect is moved forward to prospect status, they *must* be *qualified*. Suspects must have and agree that they have: (1) a need for the product, (2) a desire to take action to make a product decision, (3) the authority to make the decision, and (4) the money to pay for the product. Creativity can be used in uncovering the need and in developing financial approaches to pay for the product, but authority has to be legitimate. Desire can be created and heightened by a value perspective discussion. From a measurement standpoint, management must expect salespeople to attest that a suspect has met *all* of the four points mentioned previously before assigning prospect status to that suspect. The nature of each individual client situation in regard to each point should be entered in the salesperson's information system as the data is gathered.

Prospect Handicapping System

Products and prospects, each having different characteristics that mesh at differing degrees within a handicapping system, can reveal which prospects will have the greatest probability of buying a given product and finding satisfaction using it. Sales personnel using this handicapping structure can estimate the probability of a sale and ultimate customer satisfaction. This method also serves as a reminder to salespeople of sales ingredients that may be added to the situation to increase the probability of a sale. Handicapping can be used to help salespeople organize and visualize a hierarchy of potential sales activities based on a return on investment methodology.

At any given time, there are many selling opportunities that can be pursued by salespeople. A handicapping system can be used to point out which opportunity represents the highest potential return on time invested. This keeps salespeople working on their most important opportunities – a key element in sales productivity.

Here is an example that clarifies this concept. Each characteristic is listed, from Most Important to Least Important, and a numerical value is assigned to each. Salespeople, along with management, will need to develop their own grid for their own particular products and clients and to establish appropriate numerical credit given to each point. Again, the function here is to help prioritize opportunities for maximum productivity. Figure

Sales Prospecting Handicap Sheet

	Range		Rating
	Positive	Negative	This Prospect
There is a clear *need*	3	-3	2
Will definitely buy something	6	-3	4
Decision time frame	6	0	4
Our company has precise policy fit	6	-6	3
Trusts our company	4	-2	2
Size (dollar value) of policy	4	0	2
Will make the decision personally	6	-6	4
Competitive product under consideration	4	0	2
Has bought insurance before	4	0	0
Sales has cordial relationship	4	-2	-1
Can afford policy easily	2	0	0
Could buy more in future	3	0	1
This buyer can influence others	4	-2	0
Has friend or relative with our company's policy	4	0	3
	60	-24	+26

Figure 7.3. An example of a sales prospecting handicap sheet. (Insurance Company Example).

7.3 is a sample of a sales prospect handicapping scheme used by a life insurance sales group.

It can be seen that by rating a prospect against each of the categories and within the *range*, a value is given for each point. The sum of these values gives a *rating* for the prospect that can be used to prioritize sales activity based on actual potential. The prospect rated in Figure 7.3 received a rating of +26 out of a range from +60 to −24. Each industry must make its own set of categories and values and establish a range for its own business environment. Prospects with ratings above a certain value will be identified as high-priority prospects and those with ratings below that value will be categorized as having lesser potential.

Such prospect ratings should be updated continuously when changes occur in the situation.

Proposal Reviews

If the business organization can make use of a brief written proposal (written or verbal summation) for its customers, it can avail itself of a most powerful measurement concept. As mentioned in Chapter 6, some form of proposal (written or verbal summation) is always the closing focus of a buying decision. Such a proposal would be a concise summation of the customer's current situation – its problems and concerns – and a visualization of the newly proposed situation with its advantages and benefits. Some sales personnel may feel that such written proposals are unnecessary. A poorly written proposal can be a boring detriment, but a brief, well-written proposal can be a powerful tool for closing business, measuring sales effectiveness, and sales training.

First, a well-written proposal brings into clear, concise focus all the elements of the buying decision so that the prospect can picture the opportunity clearly. Writing the proposal forces salespeople to develop succinct statements of value and benefit addressing the individual points of the buying decision; they are forced to ask the prospect pertinent questions in order to develop a sales case that will be complete. By reviewing the proposal, sales management can see clearly how effectively sales personnel are developing a case for product value in each sales situation and offer appropriate suggestions to the sales force.

The requirement to produce brief but highly tailored proposals can generate initial resistance within the field sales group, but it will soon become second nature. The first proposal will require work, but those that follow will quickly become automatic. The benefits can be a new dimension in sales focus on the specific details of the customer's problem and a guarantee of not proceeding with product recommendation until the customer need is thoroughly understood.

A written proposal, as described here, is a hard-hitting, two- or three-page document written in terms of the prospect that goes to the heart of the issues, to the problems with the current approach and the clear benefits offered by the new one. Sales management should review and then co-sign all proposals. This is the quality measurement point: to ensure that a solid sales case is being made to, and understood by, each and every qualified prospect. Prospects will also appreciate the thoroughness and concern that this type of proposal indicates. Quality proposals like the one described in Chapter 5 positively differentiate the salesperson and his or her company from the competition. The benefits from this concept are many and the results are often dramatically positive. Continuous improvement will be possible over time with leadership from management.

Sales Forecasts

Sales forecasts can be used to measure how effectively each salesperson is making things happen instead of just watching things happen. For almost every sales organization, there is an industry sales cycle that management is following to track expected new sales. Forecasts generally are developed to predict who will buy, how much, and when. With a forecast level set by the sales personnel, expected actual sales across the period can be tracked. If the prospects who actually buy are not the ones on the forecast, the salesperson may not be effectively in control of his or her territory. Fortunate (and unfortunate) situations arise in every sales territory, but the majority of the situations that will result in a sale should be identifiable at forecast time – if the salesperson is effective and in control of the territory. The ability to identify the target and then hit it is the mark of a professional. To shoot the arrow and then draw the target is something less. Sales management should look for a high percentage of forecasted sales to materialize as predicted.

Buying Decisions

Buying decisions can be evaluated in retrospect to provide much more information than most sales organizations realize. All proposal situations should be reviewed to determine their outcome – why they turned out as they did. There are three possible outcomes: (1) the prospect bought your product; (2) the prospect bought a competitive product; and (3) the prospect did not buy at all.

If an inordinate number (as honestly established by personal investigations) do indeed buy, but not from your company, then there is possibly a problem with either the product, the service, or with the performance of the selling function. If a majority of proposal situations result in a sale, then selling is effective and focus can confidently be directed to the development of more prospects to increase overall sales volumes. If a substantial number of prospects ultimately do not buy from anyone, there is a possible problem with consistent qualification as these were not legitimate, qualified prospects for the product.

Selling and sales management are professions requiring a sense of realism. Sales measurements based on the previously mentioned indicators can point to individual problem areas, and each problem, once understood accurately, can usually be solved. A clear understanding of a problem often makes its solution obvious.

Customer Satisfaction Contacts

Customers appreciate concern for their satisfaction, and letters or brief phone calls from management or from sales personnel are generally appreciated. The key to this type of effort is that the correct individual be contacted and that objective facts and subjective attitudes toward the product be noted. Customers need to be assured that if they take their time to respond to inquiries or surveys, the information they provide will be acted upon.

Remember also that when customers relate their impressions of the quality of the product, they are also reminding themselves of these reactions. When their impressions are positive, this reaffirmation of satisfaction reinforces the sale. Often, valuable information can also be obtained from a phone call from vendor sales management to a prospect who did not buy from their salesperson. This can point out weaknesses in the sales effort or the product approach that will not be revealed by those who did buy.

Whether it is by mail (always with a stamped, self-addressed return card or envelope) or, better, a brief phone call from a sales manager expressing personal concern for the customer's satisfaction, the information acquired can guide quality improvement in the future. Positive comments from customers, shared with sales personnel, increase the sales group's enthusiasm for their products and their company. Customer satisfaction calls by management are an entrée for closer future contact between customers and management, with much consequential benefit. Sales personnel need to feel that management contact with customers is not a threat but part of the desired team effort building toward customer satisfaction and partnership.

Customer Acceptance Reviews

For key business customers, an annual visit by the salesperson, possibly accompanied by a sales manager, to brief an appropriate executive on the company's use of the vendor company's products or services can be most appropriate. Few vendors will show this level of concern, and it is generally welcomed. Customer executives are usually glad to be informed about pertinent activities within their organization. These briefings can have rich spin-off benefits. For instance, they can provide opportunities to compliment the customer company's personnel for assistance in developing new ideas that will lead to an enhanced relationship in the future.

Sales managers who implement this customer satisfaction evaluation technique will find that they lead frequently to a clearer insight into customer executive attitudes and future business plans as well as to discussions of products and services that might be supplied in the upcoming year. These conversations can also reveal points of low performance on both sides. Managers and salespeople must be prepared to hear, understand, and act on these. Strategy based on reality is the only worthwhile strategy. Manager-to-manager contact between vendor and customer substantially tightens the traditional supplier relationship.

Management contacts of this type should be kept at appropriate peer levels. They should always be well planned and professionally executed.

Support System Responsiveness

Support systems measurements are often quite difficult to establish. One concept that was studied by the IBM Corporation in a software development environment could have very broad and useful application in general business.[5] This study determined that when support systems with which employees work are slow to respond, the result is a dramatic decrease in productivity.

The concept has broad implications for all work situations, including sales. Employees are most productive when support functions within their organization respond in a rapid fashion to their working requirements. As delays occur in getting required information or support response, interest and concentration are eroded and productivity suffers. As the working rhythm of employees is broken, they tend to lose focus on work and engage in nonbusiness activities and conversation, which diverts the attention of other employees. The business that supplies its employees with responsive, timely support allows them to focus intensely on their work and to be dramatically more effective.

Whether it is price quotes, product literature, product information, secretarial services, or anything else, selling organizations seeking to develop better sales performance in the Quality Era must assess and improve support systems so that the sales group can perform at peak efficiency. Again, a graphing of sales support functions under the dynamic equilibrium concept can reveal support deficits. Ultimately, action and response are like a dance in which ideas and performance flow best when the business support systems respond to the employee's lead effortlessly and completely.

The function of business is to provide customers with what they want, in the form they want it, and when they want it. Sales employees are customers of the business as well. In fact, everyone who depends on another individual or department in order to be enabled in performing their work is a "customer" of that individual or department. The facilitation of a responsive work environment for sales group and other departments through automation and other support as required to produce desired response levels should become a key aspect of business systems evaluation. There is an *optimum* support level for a given function where expenditures yield the benefits of productivity. Up to that point, productivity is compromised by lack of support; past that point, money spent improving support is not recovered through a gain in productivity.[2]

Examples of response and performance graphs are shown in Figure 7.4 and Figure 7.5. Although these examples were part of a study of the creation of computer software, the principle that a rapidly responsive environment is conducive to great improvements in productivity can hold true for a sales organization as well. When pricing alternatives and other pertinent information as well as support services such as secretarial assistance are available quickly, more creative alternatives can be attempted and quality and enthusiasm will increase as a result. Such studies indicate that at a certain point for a given environment, an optimum level of support can be targeted at which quality and job focus are dramatically improved.

The quality philosophy of Deming and others emphasizes that in many business situations the performance of employees is tied more to the restrictions of the systems under which they work than to their own individual initiative in performance. In other words, the performance of the individual worker is constrained by a system that renders the worker incapable of higher performance regardless of the incentives or punishment applied.

An essential element of quality improvement is the objective evaluation of business support systems and the improvement of these to render them capable of higher quality employee output. A salesperson and his or her support structure might thus be considered a "selling system," and evaluation of the productive capabilities of that system can be made. Employee training and self-improvement are also part of a quality strategy. Quality Era

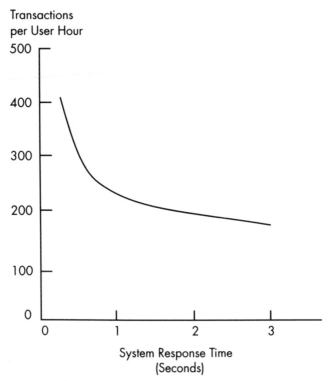

Transactions
per User Hour

Figure 7.4. The relationship between the system response time and the number of transactions a user can complete in an hour. Note that productivity increases dramatically when an optimum responsiveness is acheived – productivity falls off drammatically when it is not. In this example productivity was doubled by improving support response.

sales personnel will need to be open to personal development and come to value constructive suggestions and criticism. On the other hand, with the advent of the personal computer, many support functions have been transferred to the sales employee with the attitude of management being that salespeople no longer require secretarial and other support. The actual result is often that salespeople simply reduce their written correspondence and performance of other needed functions.

Measuring Selling Effectiveness

Sales management should have as a goal the continual betterment of the selling skills of the individuals within the sales group. Individual characteristics that are unrecognized by a salesperson can have a severely negative impact on overall performance. Many sales training methodologies are in use today, but frequently these involve only superficial measurement of the quality of the individual's sales image and techniques.

It is not uncommon for sales training personnel to observe an individual salesperson using the company's orthodox sales call methodology and yet achieving little sales impact. Salespeople's sales call efforts may be evaluated against the five categories of in depth selling effectiveness to gain insight for improvement. The five areas in which professional salespeople must demonstrate adequate capabilities are:

- Business or product premise
- Communications skills
- Product knowledge
- Sales technique
- Professional image

In observing sales calls, management should determine if the salesperson is adequately handling the subpoints within each category as discussed in the following sections in order to realistically measure personal selling effectiveness.

Business Premise

Does the salesperson engage the sales prospect in developing a realistic proposition? Was the prospect qualified by the salesperson based on realistic need? Does the salesperson tactfully outline the business responsibilities required on both sides of the relationship?

Communications Skills

Does the salesperson communicate in a concise manner with clarity and enthusiasm? Does he or she maintain the prospect's undivided attention? Does he or she hear and empathetically understand the implications of the prospect's present circumstance? Does the discussion seem to move in an organized manner toward a logical conclusion? Does the salesperson communicate with sufficiently persuasive force?

Product Knowledge

Does the salesperson appear to know the company's products, practices, policies, and resources? Are the implications and limitations of the prospect's present approach understood? Does the salesperson offer a solution that is appropriate and acceptable? Is the prospect satisfied that the salesperson's proposal represents a logically sound approach?

Sales Techniques

Does the salesperson use appropriate and penetrating questions to establish prospect need? Is desire created by dramatizing the prospect's need? Are the elements of the product solution presented so that the prospect can visualize its benefits and how they meet the stated needs? Does the salesperson alleviate the prospect's doubts in a logical manner? Is an appropriate closing action initiated defining what will happen next?

Professional Image

Is the salesperson genuinely confident and self-assured? Is the image of a mature professional conveyed in his or her appearance and manner? Is the salesperson able to create a relaxed and interesting conversational atmosphere?

For each of these broad categories, management may judge that the individual is effective or that improvement is required. It is as useful to point out to individual salespeople the strengths each naturally exhibits as to require them to focus on areas needing improvement. Sales personnel need to understand their strengths so that they can forget them and allow them to come into play naturally; attempting to keep too much strategy in one's mind while trying to behave normally toward a sales prospect is one of the chief causes of unnatural tension in sales calls. A salesperson should be given a *single* point for improvement and a methodology for working on it; that is enough. The first objective is to move the salesperson's performance to a level at which each of the five areas is acceptable. Then work can continue on developing a higher level of quality in each category. Remember, a consistent level of performance in any process must be attained before work on process quality improvement can begin. If a salesperson is judged deficient in any of the five areas, the focus should be placed on techniques that will bring his or her performance in that area up to an acceptable and dependable level.

Summary

Measurement is essential to any program of quality improvement, including those addressed to selling. The measurement standards that must be applied in sales and customer relations are of a more abstract type than those applicable to production.

Quality improvement in sales functions fits most easily under the Kaizen, or continuous quality improvement, concept. Under this methodology, a process structure is established that is determined to be capable of producing quality results if followed with commitment and determination.

Salespeople are measured on their consistency of performance within the process and less on sales results, which are often outside the control of the salesperson. This is not to imply that creativity and commitment are laid aside as employees blindly and automatically follow the process. Far from it! They must commit to the process as an efficient methodology for organizing and structuring work to yield maximum efficiency and sales productivity. For this reason, the design and structuring of the process are of the utmost importance. Processes are continually being improved by employees working with management toward perfecting the system.

The measurements suggested can be used to set beginning

performance standards within the sales continuum stages and the buying decision. Others may be used to structure procedures that will give order and method to the sales activities. By dependably establishing these measurement points, reviewing, and working on them, continuous improvement of individual and sales team quality execution will produce positive results.

References

[1] Neave, H. R., 1990. *The Deming Dimension.* Knoxville, TN: SPC Press, p. 67.

[2] Gleick, James. *Chaos.* Dove Books.

[3] Neave, *The Deming Dimension*, p. 151.

[4] Masaaki, *Kaizen*, pp. 16–17.

[5] IBM Corporation, The Economic Value of Rapid Response Time, GE20-0752. White Plains, NY, 1982.

Notes

1. The concept of *kaizen* emphasizes quality innovation on a continuous basis rather than at predetermined intervals. The institution of small but continuous improvements will, over time, produce great cumulative quality improvement.

2. Readers familiar with the Taguchi Loss Function will find that this quality concept applies well to the sales support optimization being discussed here.

CHAPTER 8

PRODUCT POSITIONING AND COMMITMENT TO VALUE

As a modern business manager, one of the more difficult aspects of charting the course toward quality is defining and understanding the term "quality" itself. We all have a sense that quality implies a degree of excellence and fitness for use, but upon attempting to give quality an incisive definition, we encounter difficulties; quality means different things to different people. The term is sometimes also used in varying degrees in reference to certain features of a product rather than as a label for the whole product.

When used to refer to internal business functions and to customer service, "quality" can have its own range of meanings. Upon reaching one level of quality, other dimensions of potential improvement become visible and satisfaction with the level attained is less than anticipated. Things can always be made better, but is perfection ever really achievable? Quality has been defined as *anything that can be improved*.

The concept of quality will always require measurement against some standard, and this standard will continually change as the capabilities of industry change and as the sophistication of customers increases. *Customer delight must ultimately be the standard of quality measurement.*[1] This means that from every aspect and in every instance of use the product will be dependable and give complete satisfaction to the customer. In this attempt to satisfy customers, the business must forever sacrifice its own ability to be satisfied with its present level of performance.[1]

Customer Delight

In the Quality Era more than ever, all strategy and execution must be performed with the objective of delighting the customer. There is, however, a new and broader concept of the term "customer" required. Certainly of overriding importance is the objective of delighting the customer to whom we sell our products. It is the customer who has the ultimate power over business success. This customer, in choosing not to buy our products, can cause us to go out of business. We must first and foremost constantly respect this customer's concept of quality.

But the Quality Era calls us to broaden our view of the customer. Customers of the Quality Era must be considered to be any individual, department, or business with whom we deal, whether it is to buy, sell, or supply support. The customers of the Quality Era are all those with whom we have dealings, because all of these dealings and their quality performance affect the quality that will be delivered to and perceived by the customer.

Quality, therefore, must take on the aspect of an habitual philosophy or mindset under which we carry on all interaction, not just something applied to products and omitted in other areas of business.

Competition Will Necessitate Quality Focus

The intensity of competition from increasingly improving products and from competitors whose business survival is dependent on differentiation through quality will yield increasingly higher levels of apparent value. We are entering a global market in which our traditional, parochial view of competition cannot comprehend the levels of sacrifice that may be made by international competitors to win in the new marketplace. National business strategies may well be based on survival, not just on making a profit. The competitive arena of a global market may see success elevate some nations and their people to elite living standards while the losers may be relegated to Third-World status, if they're not already there.

In the global race for economic success, cultural differences that would normally cause communication problems that would make selling outside these cultures difficult will instead engender creativity in creating products that will speak for themselves in terms of "quality."

The Japanese penetration of the American automobile market is a narrow example of what may appear more broadly. Having little intimate knowledge of American culture and language, the Japanese studied with *humility* and in intricate detail every advantage and flaw of domestic American automobiles and set about to offer to Americans vehicles that in terms of reliability, longevity, driveability, economy, and service far exceeded the current offerings of auto manufacturers in the United States. When offered at a lower price than American automobiles, a new value picture resulted that "spoke" to American customers and delighted them. They told other customers of their satisfaction, thus becoming nonsalaried salespeople for the Japanese products.

It is interesting to consider that by an extraordinary focus on quality required by a perceived difficulty in marketing in the traditional American fashion, the Japanese actually found a more cost-effective method of selling by channeling potential marketing money into product quality at a lower price that increased customer value and delight – a new selling concept. The Japanese, of course, used American automobile salespeople to sell to Americans, but the quality strategy mentioned above effectively overwhelmed impressions of "foreign" and "untrustworthy."

The business quest for excellence in employee performance, suppliers of components, raw materials, tax advantages, and so forth are disassociating modern corporations from their traditional national allegiance and producing business organizations that must search the world for the best "ingredients" for yielding a final quality product at the lowest price. Comprehensive business quality strategies are now driving international strategies.

A "quality" product – one that delights the customer – can be sold successfully at a higher price than the competition can sell an item of lower perceived quality. Therefore, making products of high quality at the lowest possible cost and then selling them at a higher but acceptable price is the key to maximizing profit. Another way of stating this old principle of profit making is "buy low, sell high." In some situations, a product of the highest quality might not really be necessary and customers can purchase the product at a price that is in line with its lower relative quality, thus gaining acceptable utility at a price that delights them. In this case, it is not the quality of the item that is producing customer satisfaction but the price.

All products will have a mix of perceived quality and price that, in the mind of the customer, results in a reaction that can range from outrage that so little is priced so high to delight that so much is available for so little. This interaction of price and level of quality or usefulness forms a *value* picture. This is a unique perception developed by each customer based on his or her own unique perception of the product's applicability in meeting the individual need and in consideration of the price being asked in exchange.

The term "price," in its Freudian connotation, conveys a sense of sacrifice or loss, and indeed, a purchase is a sacrifice of one thing to gain another.[2] Customers decide based on their perspective of value whether they will gain by a sales transaction. Salespeople can alter this perception and thus increase the probability of a sale by personalizing product utility in relation to the particular customer. This is a function that noninteractive marketing methods do not perform reliably. It is the reason that selling performed by salespeople will probably remain a valuable component of the marketing mix. Perception of price can also be changed by salespeople who can inject alternate methods of looking at and meeting the required financial conditions of purchase.

Salespeople, therefore, through being able to shape the perception of both usefulness (quality) and price (sacrifice), leverage the perception of value in the mind of the customer. If the product is shown to be more useful than at first supposed, then its price can be seen as more reasonable. If the price can be shown to be less of a sacrifice than first assumed by the customer, the perception of value increases. The customer is delighted over value when feeling that he or she will be getting a lot for a little – in other words, "a good deal."

Value Levels

Personal selling can relate product value to a customer from a variety of perspectives, and products need to be designed with these approaches in mind. Some potential value strategies might include:

Price	Features
Low price	Simple, straightforward, no frills function
High price	System solution product plus installation, training, and support services
Higher price	Longer-life product with low maintenance
Highest price	Absolute reliability and longevity, high trade-in (lowest net cost)

The salesperson must be capable of presenting alternative perspectives of product value and interactively applying these to the individual customer. The customer's view of value so derived should be based on the best value perspective possible for that individual customer.

Effective selling can have a profound effect on the customers' perception of value and on their buying behavior, but ethical selling and lasting customer relationships are built on the perceptions of value created at the time of sale that persist and grow stronger as the product is used. Products can, however, be designed so as to communicate their quality aspects more visibly and thus assist in their selling. They can also be designed, as everyone is aware, so that they superficially appear to offer a level of quality that they do not deliver in reality. The competitive level of quality demanded of the successful business of the Quality Era will not be superficial but deep and genuine.

The product successes of the Quality Era will be designed carefully to meet the real needs of the customer. They will be designed with new and timely information regarding customer attitudes and desires. Successful businesses will know in advance why their products will sell and to whom. They will be designing and modifying products empathetically in concert with the mind of the customer. They will also be designing and offering products that the customer has not yet envisioned but for which the vendor company anticipates an impending customer need.[2] Businesses will use their product expertise not just to respond to stated customer requirements but to innovate to delight customers.

Will this eliminate selling? Can products be designed with such immediately obvious value that they will finally sell themselves? Probably not completely. The quality strategy of the future for a great number of businesses will consist of building quality in products and revealing that quality to customers through personal selling.

The salesperson in the Quality Era must, however, assume a broader role. Rather than presenting product value outwardly to the sales customer, he or she will also be interpreting customer value perspectives inwardly to the vendor company so that products being designed and brought to market are tailored to the customer. The selling of the past came into play after the product was made; the sales groups of the future will insure the incorporation of customer needs and desires into products that customers are anticipating because these desires were communicated effectively into the design process.

Product anticipation by customers may replace the practice of releasing "surprise" products. The analogy might be made of a customer searching for a new home that meets his or her needs on the open market in contrast to another buyer who is working with an architect to design a custom home. The salespeople of the future may well be product concept architects – value designers who, using the resources of their companies in partnership with customers, envision products and partnership structures that will have predetermined maximum value for the customer.

Nothing in business is as expensive as conceiving, designing, developing, perfecting, manufacturing, and marketing a product that does not sell. The expense of building a quality item that does not sell can be even greater, for quality is not cheap. The cost of using the best components and a new design, not to mention the reorganization of the entire production process to focus on a quality strategy, can be extremely expensive – disastrously so if the products do not sell as anticipated. It is true that production efficiencies and sales increases may result, but the business adopting a quality strategy must commit to it because they view the quality as the best strategy under which the business will face the future. Quality commitment will not solve all business problems. As Dr. Deming himself reminded one young businessman, "Be careful that you don't wind up using my quality principles to become the most efficient producer of the highest quality buggy whips!"

For those businesses that effectively adopt and implement the quality strategy, there must be a new, strengthened flow of predictive information eliminating reasons for the customer not to buy. The commitment to quality is expensive – the products *must* sell. Let's take a look at some companies that made such a commitment.

Lexus

Toyota spent years researching the automobile market before introducing its new Lexus line of luxury automobiles. Their planning and design were remarkably effective. These automobiles were also priced at approximately two-thirds that of the European luxury car competition. Consumer evaluations of the Lexus LS 400 reported no flaws in design, workmanship, or performance for this new line of autos. A new value standard for luxury automobiles was set.

Companies that have a less than comprehensive view of customer need and motivation can make expensive mistakes. Now as never before, businesses need to be sure they know why and under what motivation their products are selling. Accurate and timely information from the customer verified by in-depth understanding must guide product development. Lack of in-depth understanding of both competition and customer gathered on a timely basis can result in extremely expensive mistakes.

FedEx – Zapmail

Memphis, Tennessee's FedEx is one of the leaders in the overnight shipping industry. Upon observing that printed documents comprised a large part of the business, the company set about develop and market a service called Zapmail. Zapmail would allow a customer to enter a FedEx store and transmit documents to another FedEx store major cities across the U.S. The transmitted documents would be sent electronically and reproduced in high-quality detail at the receiving location. From there, the documents would be delivered to any location in the United States within one day. This was a significant improvement over their current next-day delivery and therefore an advantage they expected customers would appreciate and use. The product was introduced and not received well by customers, with sales of Zapmail falling far below projected levels. FedEx eventually abandoned Zapmail. What had gone wrong?

FedEx had interpreted customer desire for overnight delivery of documents as a need for faster document delivery than normal mail. Working on the theory that if overnight is good, then same-day delivery is even better, they announced Zapmail. One problem was that many customers were in reality buying the reliability of the FedEx delivery system over the reliability of postal delivery, and, in many cases, overnight was sufficient provided the documents did in fact get delivered the next day – which FedEx already did reliably. A new fax technology had also been announced that, although it provided lower quality resolution, did offer inexpensive document transmission from customer offices and used telephone line transmission at very low cost. Thus, to a degree, by misreading customer requirements, customer motivation, and competitive market changes, great amounts of money and effort were expended, with poor results.

There are many interesting and even humorous stories of companies assuming the obvious in terms of market strategy, only to find that the obvious was incorrect.

Parker Pen

After the Second World War, the Parker Pen Company found that its orders for fountain pen caps in the Far East increased. Not understanding why Asians were needing to replace their fountain pen caps, Parker investigated to find the reason. What appeared to be a quality problem turned out to have another explanation.

Western ways of business and dress had begun to replace traditional Eastern modes rapidly. Along with a desire for an authentic Western look, it was observed that many successful executives always had a fountain pen with Parker's familiar arrow clip in their shirt pocket. Fountain pens being priced beyond the reach of most hardworking businessmen of the time, they adopted the next best thing; replacement caps for fountain pens that could be purchased through pen stores. The perception of wearing this prestigious fountain pen was thus produced at a fraction of the cost of a complete pen. It is not known whether Parker later capitalized on selling pens to match its caps, but if not, they or a competitor missed a fine opportunity.

Being "Into" the Product

One consistent theme of successful Quality Era companies is that their management is "into" the product. As emphasized earlier, businesses that have an empathetic understanding for their particular customer set have a strong advantage. When this understanding springs from personal use and enjoyment of the product type, the advantage can become unbeatable. Companies directed by people who actually enjoy and participate in activities that involve the products they make, have a unique identity with the thoughts and attitudes of other customer users of the product type, and their familiarity with the frustrations produced by the deficiencies of present designs can keep their innovative ideas flowing out to customers through their products. Such companies are able to maintain a sense of personal linkage. When customers view the business founder as "one of us," they tend to view the business as smaller and more personal than its growing size would seem to dictate.

Microsoft

Microsoft owner Bill Gates, for example, has been remarkably successful in establishing and holding market domination in the personal computer software arena. Although Gates is an astute businessman, one of his key assets is that he manifests a genuine love of computer technology and is able to visualize creative innovations because he is a computer "hacker" at heart himself. He is challenged in the market by many companies managed by individuals who are not so personally involved and enamored of the product itself. Gates gives the impression of doing what he loves, which is producing innovative software. The fact that he has made billions for himself and others is more of an oblique result of that passion.

The Gates/Microsoft story is not unique. It is certainly obvious that many successful modern companies were founded by people who applied creative innovation to an existing product that they themselves used frequently. But the key point here is that the successful ones, those who found and build the great companies, tend not to switch completely to a focus on monetary gain but instead maintain a love for the product and their identity with their customer or user set. The field of business is littered with the wreckage of companies originally founded and made successful by an individual who was excited by the product itself but who later turned over management to more traditional financially oriented types only to have the business go flat and eventually decline.

Products designed, built, and sold by people who are enamored of their product and thus their work can often have the "presold" aspect mentioned earlier in this chapter. When the product is surfboards built for surfboarders by surfboarders to meet the needs of surfboarders, for example, an engagement can take place between producer and customer that is hard to penetrate by a competitor who is just fabricating surfboards but is not really "into it" personally.

Companies managed by users are also quicker to move to innovate and exploit advantages because their management has got and is constantly obtaining first-hand customer information about market requirements. Thus, decisions can be made with greater speed and without the more cautious approach of other management teams, which must do voluminous surveys and gain company-wide approval for such innovation. The financial side of business and other management structures must be functioning or the business can fail from inadequate attention to these areas. A product that is selling because it is so on target

179

customers are buying faster than it can be manufactured, is a wonderful thing to behold. The business structure people can be brought in by the boatload and given plentiful revenue from a successful product.

New Products from Old Products

These dramatically successful products do not have to be that unique. A new dimension of quality, taste, ruggedness, and so forth applied to an old product type can allow it to sell at per-unit prices that more conservative management would believe unimaginable. As evidence that there are possibly no limits to what quality can produce in terms of customer response, consider Mrs. Fields' Cookies, which built an international span of stores selling $1.00 cookies; Maglite selling quality versions of the ordinary household flashlight for three to four times the price of lower quality units; or Dunkin' Donuts, which has built a multimillion dollar business based on the lowly donut.

Customers stand ready to reward outstanding quality with their money. When a product is so differentiated by quality, perceived as a value, and lifted out of simple commodity status, it can demand remarkable prices. The minute "reasonable limits" are set by market research on what a customer will pay for a mundane item, someone will produce a higher quality version of the item and destroy those boundaries. Such products are most often developed and produced by people who love the product and dream of its ultimate quality potential.

An interesting dynamic can take hold when a product excites its producer, for then through intense thought on the perfection of the product it often moves through the level of craft to that of art. In the words of one writer, "Art grows out of craft and goes beyond it, when the worker handles his materials not, or not only, as a means of reaching a certain practical end but for their own sakes, and becomes contemplative instead of merely practical."[3]

Products of the Quality Era will increasingly attain the level of art in design and function, where the synergy of ingredients produces a customer-pleasing result due to factors well beyond the practical, functional level.

I recently heard an American business executive relate the story of a group of American Steel Company managers who were spending a week in Japan touring their steel production facilities. The Japanese had listened to the Americans' approach to sales strategies, market pricing, profitability strategy, and the like. The Japanese had seemed more to concentrate on the processes they were using to produce quality metal and the years of service that employees and management had spent focused on steel production. In his summary remarks, the ranking Japanese executive said, "We have enjoyed your visit and I think we have learned much about each other's methods. I believe we have also determined a difference in our approaches which is key: You Americans are outstanding 'business' people, but we are 'steel' people." Being "into" the product produces creative innovation. Adam Smith lists this as one of the great benefits of the specialization of labor – that workers performing a task repeatedly will naturally begin to think of and try ways to improve the task and to improve the product. Quality Era workers need the freedom to suggest and implement creative innovation. Management can lead through shared vision of their product's highest potential.

I once heard a radio discussion featuring one of the few antique harpsichord renovators in America. This gentleman had been repairing antique harpsichords for many years and had seen and repaired them all. He commented that frequently the tonal quality of the antiques was superior to modern instruments. The host asked if possibly the availability and use of higher quality wood in earlier times had been partially responsible for this difference in quality. The expert, however, made another observation. The wood used in many of the older instruments was often of a variety of qualities, sometimes giving the impression that the internal sounding boards were made of whatever the maker had around in his shop. What was remarkable, he said, was that the builders of these early instruments handled wood every day. They used only hand tools, so they gained a tactile perception of each piece of wood and how it would perform; this served as guidance for how thick or thin to tailor each piece. The "feel" for the wood guided the manufacture of the parts and their assemblage into a unit that "sang." In our day of modern manufacture, power saws cut rapidly through the grain, and pieces are forced out of the wood without the workman gaining appreciation for the "personality" of the material.

A recent television program featured several successful, innovative business people. One of these was a baker who was producing bread of outstanding flavor for the restaurant market in New York City. This gentleman was tossing and kneading the dough by hand, and as he worked, he was singing to himself. "You seem to enjoy your work," the announcer commented. "Oh, yes," he said. "Each batch of dough is 'alive'; it has its own texture when it is ready to bake. You have to talk to it – I sing to it."

Being "into" the product means having a tactile acquaintance with the ingredients. Many of the quality concepts winning customers today come from companies whose workers and managers are daily in contact with their product and its actual production. A really good cook can take mundane ingredients and produce a quality meal, but given the highest quality ingredients and managed with creativity, cooking becomes art.

It is remarkable that in all observations of people who are "into" their work, there is frequently a happiness that seems to flow from the work itself. Dr. Deming determined that one key to quality is "joy in work." As workers, management, salespeople, and customers get together in product design and production, this joy can be produced on all fronts.

Steven Covey notes in his highly successful book, *The Seven Habits of Highly Successful People*, that "everything that is produced by mankind is really produced twice – once in the mind, and then in material form." A product is first a dream – possibly a plan on paper – then a finished product. In building the dream or plan, the companies of the Quality Era will network the sales group, customers, and management to dream up products that will not be surprises but products anticipated. They will be built for, and often with, the customer. Some of their innovations will come through the ideas of the customer set; others will be developed by those who make the current product. Other

182

advances will be made possible by new technology that was not available when earlier products were designed.

When a new product offers style and quality aspects that are beyond the present capabilities of competitive manufacturers to duplicate, business success can be phenomenal. Once such products reach the market and capture the imagination of the consumer, new expectations are set and the competitors are forced to play catch-up. If the product is dramatically different from previous products that fulfilled the function, the challenge to competitors can be overwhelming as they are forced to restructure their businesses – a risky endeavor. In the Quality Era, invention – or quality innovation – becomes "the mother of necessity" and sets new levels of product expectation. Some might say, "If you build it, they may come." But if you build it *with* them, they are there – to buy as well as to sometimes help in avoiding difficulties in design and construction.

Boeing

Recently, Boeing Aircraft, in designing its new 777 jumbo passenger aircraft, decided to actively engage customers in the design phase of the new plane. As these customers reviewed the plans for the new aircraft, many useful suggestions emerged that were of great importance to the customer but had not been considered by Boeing. In one instance, as customer maintenance personnel reviewed the drawings for the 777, they noticed that the fuel input couplings were to be located several feet above the maximum height that the standard airport fueling trucks could reach. The problem was pointed out by customer personnel, and modifications were made to allow fueling at a lower point on the wing. Boeing had avoided a serious and expensive problem. Had this problem not been noticed and fixed in the design stage, no currently available service trucks would have been able to fuel the new and very expensive 777.

Other Aspects of Quality

It is implicit that a Quality Era product must fulfill its basic or minimum utility functions reliably. Quality includes how well a product fulfills these functions and the degree of style and pleasure it gives the customer. A basic flaw in performance can keep a product from "ringing true" in terms of quality.

Jaguar

For many years British Leyland Motors produced a beautiful and opulent line of automobiles under the Jaguar label. In terms of style and appearance, these automobiles were considered some of the most beautiful standard-production vechicles ever. Jaguar, however, had a poor reputation for reliability – prompting some owners to remark that their cars spent more time in the shop than on the road. The cars still sold, but not in high enough numbers. Jaguar seemed unable to improve its reputation for reliability and to capitalize on its appearance and comfort advantages. It was recently sold to the Ford Motor Company, which is addressing this issue through comprehensive redesign to improve reliability.

The Jaguar was an example of a product with certain high-quality aspects not perceived to carry through consistently in its base function (i.e., to provide dependable transportation). Inconsistent quality does not delight customers.

If quality is random, it is not quality. As one customer of my acquaintance remarked, "I can get enough trouble for free. I don't have to spend $50,000 for it." A product must not just give a quality appearance at the time of sale; it should be of solid quality, and its looks should be consistent with its performance. There is more at stake than a sale; the reputation of the business and its relationship with its customers are on the line.

Building Customer Loyalty After the Sale

Quality is apparent in the use of a product when it dependably fulfills its basic functions with a style and competence that communicates the care and concern of the manufacturer for the customer's ultimate ongoing satisfaction -down to new levels of detail. Understand that Quality Era products will thus "speak" to the customer. Are customers sensitive to small details that indicate a vendor cares? Do little things make a difference? Do small details speak to customers? They do, and they will increasingly in the future.

A Lesson from a Gas Cap

Having purchased a new luxury automobile and enjoyed its features over the first 300 or so miles of use, it came time for me to buy gasoline. I was delighted to discover that inside the cover of the gas tank access plate was a bracket to hold the gas cap while filling the tank. I have since found this to be highly useful. It is a feature I would never have thought of myself – but the manufacturer had. But further, this feature told me that the manufacturer was concerned for my satisfaction in using its product, not just in selling it to me. It struck me that few customers will fill up with gasoline prior to purchasing an automobile and will have little reason to notice that such a bracket exists until *after the sale*. Are other manufacturers ready to accept the challenge and carry the quality quest for customer satisfaction to this level? In the quality markets of the future, this level of concern for customer delight will be the norm, not the exception.

Nonperforming products are a downer for everyone, including the salespeople, who must be proud of a product to sell it with undiluted enthusiasm. A similar set of steps is required to make a product, whether it is a quality item or not. Quality methodologies are often proving to be cost-effective approaches to production. Little differences can make all the difference between the exceptional and the mundane.

The System Concept

Is the product as offered part of a "systems" answer? This is a good question for the business executive, sales manager, and salesperson. A systems answer means a *comprehensive solution* – one that handles a complete customer issue. If the product is paint, do you sell a way to apply it? What about dropcloths, thinner, brushes, rollers? What about people to do the painting? Even decorators to help select the colors? One may be concentrating only on the paint business when customers are also searching for someone to assist in planning their decor. What is the customer in the market for? What are the limits? There are some things quality in a product cannot overcome. A lack of need is certainly one of them; the lack of a complete solution to the customer's need is another.

In developing a new product, customers should assist in setting performance criteria, validating design, and estimating value. Management should also use the sales group to provide additional customer insight – to communicate not just the "yes or no" of a product idea, but the "why and why not" from their empathetically gained customer point of view. The sales organization can also introduce appropriate customers to design and development groups. It can arrange visits for design engineers at customer locations to see present products in actual use. Such actions can provide an in-depth understanding of the competition and of the vendor's products as well. A vendor may have one impression of how its products are being used; reality may reveal another.

New products should have the sales group's support and validation prior to announcement. In other words, sales personnel should themselves be pre-sold by involving them from the product's inception. The product should be designed to sell.

Quality products "speak" for themselves through heightened enjoyment of the activity the product supports and a richness of experience on the part of the customer who uses it. A quality product communicates when a potential buyer imaginatively visualizes his or her satisfaction through its use. Perceptions of quality and value are the prerogative of the customer. Customers respond positively when effort toward quality is apparent in a product. "Quality" is individually interpreted and changing constantly, but it is recognizable in a general sense. A Supreme Court justice once said of pornography, "It is hard to define, but I know it when I see it." Customers have a somewhat similar attitude toward defining quality.

Information-Based Products

Products that communicate quality will be information rich. They will incorporate innovation through design, material, construction, and customer need. Their richness of quality will be the result of the incorporation of more and more pertinent information from all sources into the product itself. The best products will be those based on the best and most current information. This will include technology, art, human engineering, safety, energy efficiency, and so forth. Such information must flow readily to Quality Era manufacturers.

Procedures need to be established whereby design and engineering personnel are kept current on techniques that are often gleaned by vendor sales personnel calling on customer companies. The old process of engineering and design setting the specifications for items and materials and then passing them on to the purchasing department to obtain at the lowest price is often a major impediment to quality innovation. In many businesses, the purchasing organization very effectively keeps visiting salespeople away from engineers and design personnel. In the Quality Era, many outside salespeople will be capable consultants whose products and knowledge can contribute to product innovation. They will possess information on materials and/or techniques that can provide major benefits throughout the business, but they must have an understanding of the needs of the customer in order to help. The salesperson who just left a manufacturing plant may have had the answer to a materials problem that engineering is attempting to solve, but the message does not get through to engineering because the mission of purchasing is to procure an older, specified item at the lowest price available. I remember a cartoon I saw once in which an orderly was addressing General Custer: "Sir—I got rid of that salesman that was waiting . . . he was selling something called a machine gun . . . I told him you already had guns and were just too busy planning this Little Big Horn campaign."

Knowledge must flow easily from vendor to customer and to all departments so that products incorporate beneficial innovation as rapidly as possible. Business managers must ask what procedures are in place to allow outside salespersons and even other levels of the vendor organizations to communicate freely with any and all of their personnel for the benefit of the business. Deming emphasized that the selection of raw materials on a lowest cost basis is a barrier to quality innovation. Traditional purchasing departments that do not understand the actual need and focus only on low-cost procurement are a barrier to the free flow of useful information into the business from the salespeople working on the outside.[3] Business must be open to teamwork and partnership with their vendors for the richness of available product knowledge to flow in and affect quality.

Summary

"Too often products have been developed because financial resources, technology, production capacity, and so forth are available. The products so produced satisfy the company's needs, and management hopes that they will satisfy the customer."[4]

The Quality Era will necessitate new levels of customer understanding pervading producer and vendor organizations. As Deming has emphasized, the customer is the most important part of the production line.[5] Every activity must be undertaken with a consideration of its impact on customer satisfaction. The fact that many of today's businesses call in outside marketing firms to evaluate their customers' attitudes is indication of a serious problem. Where are their sales personnel? If they don't understand the customer how can they be selling?! Successful Quality Era businesses will know and understand their customers. All levels of the organization will be able to state what their customers want and how the business is delivering it. The sales group will play a vital role in the flow of this new information by serving as the introductory link between customers and vendor company.

Those businesses with the newly pervasive customer-oriented philosophy will be less concerned with the competition than with the strengthening of their ability to increase their quality delivery to customers. They will be forming and strengthening linkages based on respect and product quality. Customers will find no need to search out other vendors or products. The company will be building on established quality based value, and the sales group will be communicating this value to customers and customer requirements to their company.

References

[1] Neave, H. R., 1990. *The Deming Dimension*. Knoxville, TN: SPC Press, p. 31 – 32.

[2] Ibid., p. 32.

[3] Alexander, S. 1933, *Beauty and Other Forms of Value*. London: Macmillan and Company, p. 18.

[4] Masaaki, *Kaizen*, pp. 52–53.

[5] Neave, *The Deming Dimension*, p. 27.

Notes

1. Deming point #1: consistency of purpose.
2. Harlan Caruthers, College of business Administration, University of Tennessee.
3. Deming point #4: eliminate the selection of suppliers based on lowest cost.

CHAPTER 9

QUALITY CONCEPTS OF LEADERSHIP AND MOTIVATION

The pursuit of a quality strategy challenges management and all employees, including the sales group, to maintain an unrelenting focus on performing their work with new levels of genuine commitment. Commitment is the factor without which everything falls back to mundane levels, where attention to detail and the creative edge is lost. Commitment focuses the individual on his or her task with a determination to better past performance. Commitment must stimulate the creative capacities of all employees and thus the entire organization. Those companies that fail to enlist each employee to pursue quality goals with committed energy will be at risk in the market and will miss the exhilaration of high accomplishment.

A business strategy of differentiation through quality, more than any other strategy, is related to the concept of "critical mass." A majority committed to quality can pull the organization toward total commitment, but if most employees and management remain skeptical and uncommitted, quality initiatives will falter and even become counterproductive. Therefore, executive leadership must be apparent and unswerving. All can be lost if the new path is not followed with determination and resolve.

The benefits of a successful move to quality can be enormous. Employees, including salespeople, who discover new dimensions of pride in company and joy in work never wish to return to the former state. The business itself is thus transformed. New sources of confidence and optimism lie in doing the extraordinary or the previously impossible. In a shared vision can lie the highest level of human motivation, but a critical mass of commitment is necessary to reach this vantage point.

The "new" theories of total quality management deal at their foundation as much with pervasive attitudes as with improved production processes. As perspectives are adjusted, clearer paths to the quality objective come into view. In attempting to build quality performance, management must be willing to consider and incorporate subjective concepts of work and management that are capable of underpinning quality in production and sales. In craftsmanship itself, the easy way is often not the quality way. It is basic human nature to attempt first to solve problems with a moment's thought and a bigger hammer, and management is not excepted from this tendency. Quality development will require incisive planning and a scalpel. Both planning and innovation must always be undertaken with an adherence to the philosophy of quality. It is this call to a changed philosophy that most challenges today's often pragmatic executive management and causes difficulties with the implementation of quality programs.[1]

A New View of the Situation

Deming believed that most employee productivity and quality problems are due to inadequate business and production systems that are themselves incapable of enabling the desired levels of efficiency and quality. Deming states that workers, not having the ability or the authority to change the "system," simply resign themselves to doing their best.[1] In this system workers are following the old adage, "Theirs is not to reason why; theirs is but to do or die." Employees with this attitude tend to labor without the job focus that yields creativity and to shy away from transmitting new ideas for improvement upward to management.[2]

The insights that lead to quality innovation through system change are not always immediately apparent. Workers can often list factors that cause inefficiencies in their particular job function but cannot always identify the source or suggest comprehensive solutions. Employees do not have the vantage point of management to see the entire span and scope of a process with its departmental and worker interactive components. Individual workers, including salespeople, do not have the authority to change complete systems within the business; only management has that authority. Management commitment alone can perform global redesign so that processes capable of ensuring quality are implemented.

Deming stressed that existing systems or processes limit workers' performance because most are either not stable or incapable of being stabilized and are therefore subject to a stream of extraneous random errors that put workers and management in continual reaction mode. Employee results are therefore almost totally at the mercy of these unstable and inadequate systems. It follows, then, that under these antiquated systems the structure of awards, merit pay, employee ranking, and the like is misdirected. Deming estimated that 94 percent of productivity results from the frequently inadequate system within which employees must work, and that only the remaining 6 percent is controlled by the workers.

The feeling, prevalent among many salespeople, that "it is better to be lucky than good," is thus very astute. Management, teamed with employees, must structure business systems and processes for the Quality Era that eliminate luck (i.e., erratic results) and empower workers to be as good (i.e., as proficient and efficient) as their abilities make possible. These principles are equally true for the sales function.

Much expertise is currently focused on developing total quality concepts through business systems analysis and improvement. Many of these utilize employee observations and suggestions developed through quality circle concepts. Interdepartmental dialog is being fostered through these approaches with representatives of involved departments joining in task force or team evaluations of business systems. The goal of such activities is to develop and implement systems and processes that will enable the desired level of quality performance and to foster a shared vision of quality objectives that can pervade the company.

Quality Innovation for the Sales Group

The sales organization is often caught up in these interdepartmental activities. As suggested earlier, the sales group can appear to have a somewhat disjointed relationship with the more central-office-based business functions dedicated to designing, delivering, and collecting. Salespersons, often being out in the field performing a customer advocacy role, can appear detached and even adversarial to the central departments.

In quality-focused interdepartmental dialog it must be remembered that the sales organization is often the group closest to the mind of the customer. Salespeople can provide customer insight based on conversations with, and observation of, customers. They can often arrange for actual visits and interviews with customers by representatives from other departments seeking better methods of service.

All innovation and planning in Quality Era business must be performed with an understanding of how the new concepts of operation being considered will be perceived by customers. One really effective way of finding out how customers will react to an innovation is to ask them. If, as Deming says, everything should start with the customer – then start with the customer!

Problems to Avoid in Focusing on Quality

Many of the business functions open to quality improvement can be addressed by simple and obvious solutions. One frequent complaint of employees about the quality meetings and lectures prevalent in business today is that they lack a proportional relationship to the problem under consideration. Quality sessions can become, if conducted without appropriate perspective, one of the "systems" that is hampering worker efficiency. Meetings should not be called to solve simple and obvious problems. It is inappropriate to convene a meeting to determine whether phones should be staffed to ring either three or four times before answering. Planning sessions can interfere with employee work. Inordinate time spent accomplishing what could be achieved in a brief, open discussion or by management leadership causes the entire concept of quality improvement to take on a negative bureaucratic connotation with employees.

Quality focus meetings and programs should be planned and implemented so as to demonstrate quality themselves. Too often they are not so designed; they cause employees to fall behind in their work and make management appear inept. Employees often suspect that midlevel managers simply follow orders from above, no matter how ridiculous and inefficient. Poorly focused quality meetings have now confirmed this to millions of employees. The problem is exacerbated by the fact that employees who protest that their company's quality initiatives are ineffective are often accused of being against quality. To be against "quality" is to be against management, its policies, and against the longevity and improvement of the business. Employees who recognize the obvious and voice it can become pariahs within the company, regardless of the truth of their observations.

Management would do well to inject quality discussion and quality programs carefully and to orchestrate them sensibly. Pervasive quality is not a commodity to rush out and buy; it is a new way of thinking that requires new perspectives of practicality.[3] Many simple things can often be done to improve and stabilize existing systems and processes if managers will simply structure opportunities for the comfortable and informal interchange of ideas with employees. Employees must not be put in the position of feeling forced to tell management what it wishes to hear. It is often the communications of most crucial importance that managers appear not to wish to hear. When managers can permit a few negative comments on their quality programs as readily as they allow positive ones, they may be reaching the proper level of employee comfort required for truly productive dialog – (the two-way discussion of issues by perceived equals). As one astute manager once said, "If employees just repeat back to me what I tell them, I might as well have a group of parrots – and parrots will work for crackers."

The story is told that in one of his early speeches after assuming complete power over the Soviet Union, Joseph Stalin was outlining a new five-year plan in an address to the Supreme Soviet. At the conclusion of his speech, the audience gave the usual standing ovation. On this occasion, however, as each minister looked around at his peers and saw them applauding, the effort on the part of each minister was redoubled. The applause went on and on until it became obvious to all that whoever stopped clapping first was less loyal than those who continued. Stalin himself began to look over the audience, which heightened the tension. It is said that soon aides and assistants rushed onto the floor to prop up the exhausted arms of their particular ministers so that they would not appear unsupportive. The applause continued until Stalin left the hall. He had their attention; whether he had their commitment was not so certain.[4]

Managers working toward quality innovation must show involved leadership in systems improvement and gain the genuine attention and commitment of the employees. It is in the effort to establish consistent employee commitment that many of today's quality programs are breaking down. Employees sense that management itself is attempting to pursue quality improvement without an understanding of or commitment to the underlying philosophy. The remainder of this chapter deals with building a real commitment on which to base sensible quality programs. Having done this, all areas of the business, including the sales organization, can approach new levels of performance.

Keys to Success in Quality

Quality initiatives of the future – those that propel the successful companies – will be built on a consistent quality philosophy, out of which will flow approaches that consistently ring true with management and employees. This philosophy will permeate the minor aspects of business as well as the large. One executive observed, "You can tell a lot about a business office by 'accidentally' dropping a memo on the central office floor area and watching to see if it will be picked up by the employees passing by." A successful Quality Era business is built on the interaction of people who care and reinforce each other to produce a quality result. Their focus is on continual improvement of the business, on team success.

Broadened motivational aspects, which are the true foundation of quality, must parallel and enable the required systems innovations. When all individuals and departments of a company are sincerely asking what they can do to improve the overall performance of the company based on service to customers, management has achieved the first plateau in the quest for quality. Everyone must be focused on the desired *team result*, not on personal issues. Each employee must perceive that the realization of his or her own objectives is clearly linked to the company's achieving its objective of delighting customers.

Shared Vision

As Deming stated so often, "Quality is made in the boardroom." Quality programs must be initiated and nurtured continuously from the highest levels of business management in order for them to take hold and grow. Not only is support and commitment needed, but the support and commitment must be focused on a pervasive vision, shared by all employees, of the objectives of the business and the company's plan or methodology for reaching these goals.

Business Objective

The business objective statement sets out the business's reason for existing and its strategic approach for continued existence. Quality Era businesses can have multiple reasons for existence, such as to provide a profit for owners, to provide steady employment for workers, to provide quality products for customers, and so forth.

The second part of the objective statement might include strategy such as that outlined in the following vision statement: "We will make a profit for our owners and provide steady income for our workers by being the low-cost, high-volume producer and seller of widgets." The vision statement can grow with added strategic approach information contained in phrases such as "with the highest quality customer service." The statement of business objectives and strategy can include quite a few points but should be sufficiently limited so that it can be readily understood and remembered by all employees. Most importantly, it must be clear enough so that at all levels and in all departments employees and managers can picture the processes and attitudes that are essential based on the vision and strategy. Equally important, managers and employees can see which of the present structures, practices, and approaches are at odds with the business objective.

Everything within the business therefore becomes subject to evaluation as to its contribution to or detraction from the strategic objective of the company. Based on this perspective, management can institute processes and procedures that are in line with the stated strategy and objectives and eliminate or revise those that are not. This objective or mission statement incorporating quality strategy must become an attitude that permeates and motivates all employees, including the sales force.

Product and Company Motivation of Sales

The sales group, like any other department in a company, works most effectively when it has a clear vision of its mission. Throughout this text, we have considered a broadened vision for the sales organization. It is based on a more organized and structured selling process, and on involving the salespeople and their customers in the design and related planning for new products. The result of this activity should produce among sales personnel a feeling of ownership of products and pride in company that will increase their enthusiasm for selling. Because they have been involved in development, they should become more committed. Based on the effective market support plans that they have helped to develop for new products, they should know where the product fits in the market and how well it will perform against competition. The sales group should therefore have a clearer picture of the value offered by these products and for which customers they will have the strongest appeal. Through the handicapping system, the sales force should have guidance as to which prospects offer the most reasonable expectations of a ready sale and ultimate customer satisfaction. Because they know that the product is designed and manufactured well, they can recommend it with full confidence and without fear that their credibility and relationship with customers will be compromised.

Within many companies today, great amounts of predevelopment information on product need, pricing, and competition are gathered by the design and development groups. However, when a product is produced and released, the sales group is often not given the information that was used to support and justify the development effort. The sales organization is then placed in the position of having to rediscover this existing information, which is precisely the material they need to fully explain the product concept to customers. Salespeople should always be given detailed product development information to use in their selling efforts. Indeed, they should participate actively in generating it.

Communication between the sales group and design and development as well as the feedback of customer information throughout the sales continuum should ensure that the product aspects of the motivational picture are complete. But there are other aspects to sales management and leadership that should be understood. Management must motivate both individual employees and corporate teams to build a spirit of commitment that pervades the entire organization.

Salespeople are hired and trained to empathetically understand the customer's needs. They utilize this faculty in selling, and it cannot be turned off when observing the activities and actions of their own company. Products and policies must be credible for them to feel fully confident. They will sense an inconsistency between talk about quality that does not translate into concurrent action.

Consistency in the Pursuit of Quality

The pursuit of quality will require consistent focus throughout the organization. This is possibly the most difficult aspect of the quality innovation process. The challenge to management of getting everyone on board at the same time can seem almost impossible, but it must be done if quality efforts are to succeed. Employees will be sensitive to other departments and to personnel who are not committed. If quality measures are implemented erratically or are not consistently nurtured and monitored, they quickly revert to "business as usual" status. A change in methods and systems is essentially a change in habits. Habits are hard to break for individuals. To change the habits of a large group of people simultaneously can seem to be impossible. The composite incentive structure must be capable of accomplishing this.

Incentive Structure

Any manager looking out across his or her organization and its current performance sees an *equilibrium* established as the result of the existing incentive and enablement structure. To lead the organization toward a new level of quality consciousness and commitment, management must change the incentive structure and/or the enablement structure, thus shifting this equilibrium. A business is getting, in effect, what it is asking for – not verbally but realistically. By looking at the components of these two structures, a plan can be developed to change each component and to shift the equilibrium toward the desired objectives.

Enablement Structure (Can Do)

Throughout this text, we have dealt with the qualitative structural improvement of the sales process. The buying decision and the sales continuum approaches offer a structured methodology that allows employees to perform at a higher level of consistent quality in selling. The focus must also be on enhancing information flow to and from customers into and out of the vendor business at each stage of the sales continuum. Barriers to the internal utilization of the sales group may be addressed by enhancing the understanding of the sales personality and the selling function by the other departments, as covered in preceding chapters.

Through the establishment and support of the structured selling procedures outlined previously in this book, salespeople can be measured on the consistency of their efforts within the defined sales process as well as sales results, which they cannot always control. This can improve morale and allow for continuous improvements of both the process and individual skills.

Systems modification should be paralleled with training and personal development to strengthen each individual salesperson's capability.

Motivation Structure (Want To)

Current quality improvement programs often do not consider the motivation of employees to participate at an increased level of commitment. Employees, including salespeople, will attend quality sessions and participate when ordered to do so, but it is a deeper, genuine commitment back at the job that will produce the quality results desired. Too often, quality programs do not have desired results because motivation is the missing ingredient. Management must ask itself, in complete honesty, these questions: If these employees participate with renewed commitment in moving the company toward quality objectives, what will be *their* reward? Do *they* understand and perceive its value? A customer does not buy if insufficient benefit is seen; employees will not buy into a quality program unless they are effectively sold as well. Desire is the energy to take action. Changing habits is action; employees must have a desire for quality. Management leadership must build that desire.

Altruistic Motivation

Some motivation may be derived through exhorting employees to care for the longevity and profitability of the company; noting that these can only be ensured by innovations to improve quality and competitive stance. Such motivation may, however, be more a long term result of quality initiatives than an initial prime motivating force. Only when a genuine trust of management motives and respect for its leadership toward quality have been established will the altruistic factors of pride in work and company begin to have full effect. Employees, including sales, often believe that only management benefits when they work harder and produce more under slogans and exhortations. As Deming points out slogans and exhortations are counterproductive – hollow words – when the real issues of quality lie in restructure of the systems and processes restricting quality performance. Management must regain the trust and involvement of workers and that make the first series of moves to reengage employees. When employees gain confidence that management is genuinely committed to positive change and regard for employees the latent energies of pride in work and loyalty to company can be unleashed. In many companies workers are skeptical – their current skepticism is not without foundation. One worker summed it up this way: "Company programs can be evaluated by asking two simple questions: 'Who does the work? and 'Who gets the money?' " Employees are not unintelligent. The often great disparity between executive management compensation and worker compensation in American business confirms workers' skepticism that management's motive for talking quality is a selfish one. The Japanese honor their quality philosophy by rejecting such enormous disparity in earnings. The change of habits that can energize moves to quality must utilize every facet of positive motivation that management can generate.

Self-Interest Motivation

Management should always expect employees to respond best to self-interest motivation. In essence, all employees will ask, "What's in it for me?" This attitude should not be surprising when it is voiced by salespersons and other employees or when we discover it to be a consistent characteristic of our customers. Two hundred years ago Adam Smith observed that the "selling" of any item must be based on the advantages it offers to the individual.[2] We might hope that the world will one day function on a more altruistic level, but that day has not arrived. Machiavelli said that "the way men actually think and behave is so different from how they ought to think and behave that any prince [manager] who bases his plans on how men *should* act is *doomed* to destruction."[3] Self-interest motivation is natural and the most powerful form of inspiration. It requires more in-depth work and understanding on the part of management than the altruistic brand, but it is in actuality many times more lasting and effective.

One form of self-interest motivation is, of course, fear. Managers can and have issued edicts that unless certain procedures are carried out at a certain level of quality, employees will be disciplined by having their pay reduced or by losing their job. This type of motivation has numerous detrimental effects in the Quality Era company. Threat causes fear, and fear inhibits creative thought and open communication. Dialog and creativity are at the heart of all successful quality programs and must not be inhibited. Quality is a concept that requires synergy. The fear created by threats causes workers and departments to isolate themselves and adopt defensive and even competitive stances, all of which are totally inconsistent with the teamwork and common vision that must prevail across a company in order to achieve a business focused on quality. Fear causes the vision to become one of individual survival, and teamwork changes to individual competitiveness and loss of trust. Deming has emphasized that management must erase fear to institute quality.[4]

Personal Intrinsic Motivation

All people have in common the desire for certain things, and their activities are oriented toward fulfilling these desires. Just as discussed earlier, solutions to customer needs must be presented from a personalized perspective; so must employee needs be empathetically understood and motivational solutions tailored to meet them. Just as customer understanding must be empathetically derived, so must be the employee motivational structure.

The structure called the buying decision for customers can be called the "buy in" decision when applied to employee motivation. Just as magazine advertisements are limited in their ability to interact with a specific customer to derive a custom solution, so standardized company motivational policies affect different individuals in different ways. Motivation is in essence selling. Management must sell employees on commitment to quality. The goal, as usual, is to meet or exceed the expectations of the customer (in this case, the employee) and secure genuine desire and commitment to quality initiatives.

Components of Personal Intrinsic Motivation

Reward. In 1983, a recognized public opinion researcher, Daniel Yankelovich, published an article called "Putting the Work Ethic to Work."[5] Its thrust was to outline business changes that might improve the productivity of the American worker. Its findings still have great relevance today. Yankelovich found that most workers really want to work productively and most enjoy their work. It was not a lack of desire to work that held them back. As studies were analyzed and information compiled, a picture emerged, revealing something like this: Work might be divided into two segments – we'll call them X and Y. The X component is the minimal work performance required to stay employed and not be terminated. The Y component is any effort or commitment shown above the X level. The Y component consists of any extra initiative, creativity, special efforts, and so forth.

The studies revealed that it appeared to workers that a preponderance of reward and benefits accrued from performing the X component of their jobs, and that, therefore, in terms of pay, the X hours paid much more than the Y hours. In effect, increased attention, initiative, and commitment, which are so essential to quality improvement, are not given any impetus by current compensation and incentive structures. It appeared obvious to employees that greater personal reward was achieved by performing at only the X level and not by committing any effort to Y-type activity. (Only 9 percent of workers believed that they would personally benefit from increases in productivity.)

Since altruistic motivation formed the majority of Y-level compensation, it is no wonder workers did not show more commitment to the company and toward improving productivity. Motivational structures must be tailored by management that will allow participation in the reward structure to parallel the required individual commitment and subsequent quality results. This study is, of course, simply confirmation that employee behavior is a result of the incentive structure under which the business currently operates.

Quality Era sales personnel must be motivated consistently

to commit to Y-level performance. Commission sales plans already in place in many companies focus on *sales results* at the Y level. In the age of quality, where a long-term customer relationship is the desired result, a structure more designed to compensate for excellence in establishing and maintaining such relationships will be in order. The first sale might not be "valued" as highly as the long-term stream of business resulting from the relationship. Compensation structures must be envisioned in which the long-term dependable execution of the sales processes is compensated as heavily as the sales revenue component. Incentive and reward structures must be added for the contributions made by the sales group to product design and internal improvements.

To have a sense of pride in company and joy in work, employees must feel that they have control over their performance. Deming and other Quality Era experts have emphasized that chance has much to do with performance results in many present level business situations. This is also true for salespersons. Under the new concepts of quality, sales employees should have compensation plans under which they are compensated partially for quality execution of sales processes.

Of course, results are what count ultimately. But it is the faithful, disciplined, and committed attention to execution of a *quality-capable process* that will produce the most substantial *team* results. Current incentive structures for salespeople actually create a diversion of attention away from the process and its execution by falsely assuming that occasional and dramatic sales successes must have been due to an effective process. This often is *not* the case.[5]

When we provide incentives for salespeople based on fortuitous events, we are encouraging them to focus on tactics of luck and positioning rather than on improving their skill and methods. We are encouraging the sales prima donna concept of dramatic personal sales capability. The *sales process* and its *execution* is where management's attention should be. If the process is right and it is executed faithfully and with commitment, then the *team* result will ultimately exceed the sum of a few stellar performances turned in by sales superstars. It is the superstar salesperson's process and methodology that should be studied and incorporated into a team-executable strategy. Everyone can faithfully execute a good, process-based sales strategy. Thus salespeople are given control over what they are able to effect. This concept is a key to continuous quality improvement.

Recognition. From our previous discussion of sales, we determined that the sales organization is often the primary interface between the customer and the vendor company. Sales groups often appreciate recognition in the form of praise from management, especially in the presence of customers. They also appreciate recognition accorded them in internal memos and in articles outlining their achievements in companywide news media. Salespeople are charged with making things happen, and the recognition that they have performed their function well means much to them. Significant accomplishments, when appropriate, should be confirmed from top management by letter and personal contact. Recognition through formal and informal luncheons at which salespersons have conversational interaction with company executives without the presence of midlevel management accomplishes several functions, including making the salesperson feel appreciated and permitting an unfiltered view of sales reality to be shared with top management. Salespersons working toward promotion to management can also be viewed by executive management in these instances. Also, creative suggestions and offers of support can flow from management to the individual salesperson. A high percentage of sales personnel are interested in personal and professional development. The ability to interact with higher level executives and gain insight into their style and concepts is often highly valued. Upper management often sets too low a view of the value salespersons place on such contact.

At a companywide sales awards conference in San Francisco, one of IBM's top salespeople was invited to dinner with a divisional vice president and his staff. The topic over dinner was, of course, business and the perspective of the salesperson on various market issues. At the conclusion of dinner, the vice president apologized to the salesperson for monopolizing his evening while he could have been out "with the guys" enjoying the San Francisco night life. The salesperson honestly responded that most members of the sales group would have preferred the option of dinner and informal interaction with top company management to the San Francisco night life. It was a sincere comment. Perhaps a visit to some of the evening's tourist attractions by the vice president and the sales group together would have been the best alternative of all.

Personal Growth.   Salespeople frequently read materials that they hope will enhance their professionalism and their sales performance. A person attempting to grow often seeks, appreciates, and benefits from constructive comment and criticism. Constructive suggestions from management must be given in the mildest terms unless they deal with pivotal issues of actual job performance. It is difficult for management to make any critical comment without creating an inordinate reaction. The right for management critique should be earned through actual field observation of the sales activity.

Honest attention by a manager to the personal development and progress of the salesperson as a professional is a highly satisfying thing. The most useful analogy to a sales manager in the Quality Era may well be that of the manager of a professional athlete. Such a manager is at all times interested in arranging the best opportunities for success for the athlete – ensuring that the situations where he or she is placed to perform will make fullest use of their unique and individual talents and providing development and high chances of success. Such a manager is interested in the cultivation and growth of the salesperson and spends time planning and structuring that development.[6]

Sales employees respect managers who can make genuine contributions to their growth and, when appropriate, offer them sincere compliments. The concept of a manager who is looking out for the salesperson while the salesperson looks out for sales production is a comforting one for the salesperson. The "boss" who commands performance instills fear and incomplete commitment, which is contradictory to quality objectives. Sales employees derive genuine personal benefit from management that takes sincere interest in their professional development. The company that provides such management develops loyalty and commitment in its employees.

Achievement. Achievement in terms of sales motivation means that the individual's accomplishments are noted and remembered. Salespeople, of all company personnel, are aware that sales can go up and down and that yesterday's hero can become tomorrow's goat. Salespeople simply want it remembered, when adversity comes, that they are accepted and proven by their past accomplishments and that the company believes that they are continuing to contribute through consistent professional effort. Likewise, when individuals have accomplished sufficient growth in sales capability and in their understanding of company policies and structure, and are ready to move to a position of higher responsibility, they will wish to be told that their achievements have been noted and that they have met and exceeded the requirements of the job assigned.

Some salespeople will not want to go into management. These persons should be encouraged and allowed to improve and grow further in the sales function itself. Such individuals can be given broader responsibilities and elevation in title and pay to denote achievement while maintaining the functional sales role. As broader roles of selling unfold directed at major partnership structuring, experienced salespeople may have almost unlimited growth within the sales function. The Quality Era will allow and encourage individuals to occupy the positions in which they will be best able to make their maximum contribution. The Quality Era company will provide methods for allowing individuals to remain in the place which they choose as most appropriate for themselves. The artificial expectations of making a natural progression into management may well come to be recognized as having the potential to move an individual from a productive place to one in which he or she is less productive and less happy. The employee who becomes a manager in the company of the Quality Era should be the individual who can best fulfill, and desires to fulfill, the role of manager.

Motivation that leads to quality in business will focus on creating a work environment that is pleasant and rewarding. Employees should be able to enjoy their work and to take pride in their accomplishments. Management will facilitate, encourage, and guide with constant attention to improving processes. The work environment must offer very open communications between all levels of employees. Some Japanese firms are already moving toward work settings in which the executive manager's desk is at the center of an open working situation surrounded by other employees. This is in stark contrast to current hierarchical management structure, which means increased management isolation from the workers so prevalent today in American business. The Japanese have come to feel that such free and open communications enlists everyone in the process of quality innovation.[7]

Not only does open communication have quality improvement implications, it has motivational ones as well. A recent article in *The Wall Street Journal* dealt with a study of workplace motivation that found that the most wanted and desirable aspect in the work environment was open communication. The ability to interact openly and productively with other workers, including management, is a cornerstone of quality development. It makes everyone feel a valued part of the organization, encouraging pride in company and joy in work.

Leadership versus Management

Open office concepts and the ability to communicate freely also encourages teamwork and brainstorming, which leads to productivity and creativity. Management isolation in the Quality Era can be counterproductive. There is a spirit of humble responsibility that seems to pervade the thinking of many Japanese executives as they pursue Quality Era objectives. Historically, western management has appeared to grow more aloof and distant with increasing monetary success. If not accepted with humility, success can produce the very seeds of destruction – pride, arrogance, separation, and the loss of empathetic identity with employees and customers. American management would do well to remember an observation made by Alexander Solzhenitsyn that "pride tends to grow on the human heart like lard on a pig."

Sales managers of the Quality Era must view their employees as their customers. This implies an empathetic understanding in order to engage commitment by helping the salesperson to see that a commitment to quality is in line with his or her own personal goals. Employees often need assistance from management in perceiving that they have within their reach the ability to achieve their own goals of job satisfaction, increased earnings, and personal advancement. The key to this is management's understanding that different employees will want different things and place different values on different options – just as customers do.

Management involvement offers employees the advantages of a detached view and a realistic opinion of circumstances (i.e., mentorship). Employees can become frustrated by their inability to make improvements in their work situation. The observations and assistance of management, because they are not so intensely and directly involved, can often cut through this maze and be a genuine help to the employee – not because managers are smarter than employees, but because they are more detached and can see issues from a different perspective.

Maximizing Motivation

The effective managers of the Quality Era will work for their people while the people work for the company. Effective management begins with an empathetic understanding of the individual, the cultivation of potential by training, and with the careful placement of that individual in a business assignment that is suited for him or her. This will require that management understand that each individual employee is a valuable resource. Employees who do not have commitment to bring to the job will not be retained. Business will not have the luxury of dealing with the less-than-committed. The pursuit of quality is serious business. Employees will need to take responsibility seriously. Pride of organization and pride in product will be some reward, but other tangible compensation must also ensue.

Nothing so dilutes the justifiable pride of a team as the inability of management to deal with poor performers. One of the aspects that will naturally follow in the Quality Era is that for companies and for individuals there will be consequences for poor performance. The destructive mentality that allows employees to be left in positions for which they either cannot do the work or do not wish to do the work leads to wasted time and wasted productivity for the company and the individual. Individuals who are misplaced in a company, or in a work situation, will not be successful. Respect for that individual necessitates that he or she be given the opportunity to be successful in another assignment, possibly outside the company. This is the proper step for both the company and the individual.

Employees being assigned to new positions need to bring with them a majority of the skills required to do the job. Management should not promote an individual until that individual is performing above the requirements of the current job. It is unfair to the employee to be placed in a position for which he or she is unprepared. It demoralizes the individual so "promoted" and it is destructive to the development of the employees who report to them and depend on them for their own development and management. Pursuit of quality is a pursuit of honesty. Those moved ahead to positions of responsibility must be clearly worthy of promotion in the eyes of all. As with customers in the buying decision, the credibility of executive management and its reputation for astute judgment must be preserved. This is nowhere more visible than in its management of personnel.

In building motivation and securing commitment from sales employees, several important contributions can be made by the immediate manager. Most important of these is to understand that the employee is an individual with unique personal needs and objectives. Open and trusting discussion of these personal goals and the suggestion of others by genuinely concerned management facilitates mutual trust. This builds employee commitment and trust in management to a new and higher level.

Management that is reliable and that maintains ongoing, open, and mutually beneficial communication with employees can help them see the often unseen "critical mass" potential in both sales situations and personal opportunities.

Critical Mass

Critical mass can be applied to more than atomic reactions. The concept is that for an explosion to take place, the necessary ingredients must simultaneously be brought together. As applied to sales situations, it can mean that a great potential for opportunity is at hand if the ingredients are recognized and brought together properly. As mentioned earlier, management can take a different view of individual situations and assist in the creative structuring and positioning so that maximum benefit is realized. Management also has resources to add to the situation to further ensure the beneficial "explosion." As pointed out in our discussion of the handicapping concept, a variety of ingredients contribute positively or negatively to a sales outcome. The support of management in structuring the existing ingredients – and in adding any that are missing – can ensure the most positive of outcomes for the employee. The result is respect, loyalty, and commitment.

Let's consider the story of Mike Ward, a very effective salesperson. Over the past four years, his manager, Paul Johnson, had seen him develop into a true professional. Paul knew that Mike had the trust of his customers and the respect of his peers. He was a solid and dependable part of Paul's sales team. Paul also knew that Mike aspired to be a manager some day. Because of their conversations concerning Mike's desires for the future, Paul knew that Mike wanted more challenge and also more earnings. Mike and his wife Janet were expecting their second child, and the apartment in which they lived, though adequate, would soon be too small for their growing family. Mike was fairly well positioned saleswise for the quarter, with business expected from two new accounts that could close at any time. The customer management had not reached a final decision, though Mike had presented a clearly beneficial business case. He was sure they would both buy – eventually.

Paul also knew that Bill Reed, the divisional sales manager, was due to visit their sales office the next week and had voiced a desire to meet some of the local customers. Paul asked Mike to drop by the office that afternoon for a short chat.

"Mike," Paul asked, "what is the real situation with the two new accounts you are working on?"

Mike responded that one wanted a special-delivery consideration and the other needed a support engineer who was currently dedicated to another project. "If we can get these for them, will they sign up?" Paul asked.

"I believe that's what's holding them back," Mike replied.

"I'd like to contact your executive in each of these accounts by phone if that's all right with you, Mike. I may be able to get involved and help you close this business."

"That's fine," said Mike. "It's been hard for me to talk to either account this week – they are having meetings."

The next morning, Paul briefly reviewed both of Mike's proposals and, with a clear understanding of what Mike was recommending and why, he made several phone calls. One was to clear the delivery situation and the other was to secure a very talented engineer from their midtown location.

Then Paul made the customer phone calls. John Willis was in meetings all week, but when his secretary informed him that Mike's manager was on the line, he took the time to talk. Paul apologized for the interruption but was quite pleased to relate that as a result of Mike's tireless efforts the company had found a way to grant the delivery provision requested. Could Mr. Willis sign the agreement next week to confirm the delivery? Willis agreed and said he would be glad to see Mike on Tuesday morning. The second call obtained similar results, with a meeting scheduled for Mike to get the other order signed, also on Tuesday.

Bill Reed's visit to the sales location was a great success. As "chance" would have it, Mike was assigned to play host to Bill. Bill "just happened" to be in on closing two new contracts for the company. He heard ample praise for Mike's sales coverage and dedication from these two new customers and from Paul, who had already briefed him about Mike. Bill Reed also met with Paul, who requested his authorization of a pay increase for Mike. Bill also stated that the division was planning a series of management development classes in the fall at headquarters, and that he would certainly approve Mike's attending.

Quite often, the ingredients of a real success are lying about all over, but they must be brought together to the benefit of all concerned. Just as in the story about Paul and Mike, the role of management in orchestrating, facilitating, and ensuring success generates maximum benefit for the team. Is there any doubt that Mike's loyalty and commitment to Paul and the company is stronger than it would be if he had simply attended a called meeting and listened to a lecture from Bill Reed on the benefits of company loyalty?

Loyalty and commitment are earned by the company and management. They are secured by engagement – by showing how the desires and needs of the company can be aligned with the desires and needs of each employee. The ends pursued by the employee and the company then become the same – the motivation will have become individualized.

Respect for management does not come automatically. The companies of the Quality Era should pay careful attention to the management abilities of those assigned leadership positions. Managers must know the mechanisms of the business better than their employees and be capable of creatively using this knowledge. Paul was a "front-line general." This term comes from the habit of many of history's most successful military commanders to be with their troops in the front of the battle. These commanders have felt that the advantages of firsthand observation and involvement in situations warranted their own personal inconvenience and risk.

The ability of management to make sacrifices for the personal betterment of those in their charge is a key ingredient of leadership. Employees need to feel that they are cared for and that management is not distant and unfeeling. Loyalty between employees and management is forged in the front-line situations of business. (Paul was able to confidently make a sales contact himself, but he showed respect for Mike by asking for his okay beforehand.) Salespeople are often territorially possessive. They are constantly in the process of building customer relationships, and management should not inject itself on impulse without first understanding the situation and the relationship that the salesperson is attempting to build. Management contact with customers through salespeople should increase and become more routine in the Quality Era. The sales group will become less territorial as its trust of all levels of management increases.

When appropriate, certain items that mark achievement may be selected by management and awarded to salespeople. Some of the best of these rewards are not necessarily expensive; their value to the recipient lies in the fact that his or her excellent performance has been recognized throughout the business. In terms of sales motivation, items like the corporate equivalent to a Master's jacket or a Super Bowl ring are affirmations of achievement that cannot be bought. They are unique and given only to a select few. Those who think that humans can be motivated to do great things to win such baubles are precisely correct; they can, but of course it is the achievement that is the motivation and not just the object.

The most important and meaningful awards given to salespeople are those that convey the understanding and acknowledgment that it was the unique personal capabilities of that individual that made the accomplishment possible. Possibly the most exhilarating feeling in life comes from feeling that one is being used effectively in a truly great purpose. It is remarkable how many veterans, when asked about a war, will first talk of the pain of being separated from their families and the hardships of the campaign but then will readily remark that they look back on the experience as the most exhilarating experience of their lives. They will give statements of feeling "alive" and more "awake" than at any other time in life. Under intense situations new dimensions of the self are discovered. Leadership can wake up a sleeping business.

The businesses of the Quality Era must offer salespeople the opportunity to do great things. Quality-oriented management leadership will be a genuine call to join in doing the unique and special. It is a call for a new level of service. It will offer opportunities for individuals to find new dimensions of personal satisfaction. While monetary reward should follow excellence in performance, quality is not just a strategy to be pursued to gain wealth; it is a thing to be pursued because it is the key to personal satisfaction. To do less is never to know the capabilities dormant within oneself and one's associates. Awards of the Quality Era will commonly focus on team achievements of which each individual is part. Management assumes the responsibility for the success or failure of the business through the processes and structures it establishes. Employees assume responsibility for the execution of these processes.

I am reminded of an incident that demonstrates the new level of leadership commitment to quality for business, employees, and customers. Some years ago a Japan Airline Boeing 747 crashed in Japan. The cause of the crash, which was fatal to all aboard, was a ruptured bulkhead – possibly a construction flaw. The tragedy of the crash is not the point of the story, but the reaction of the management of JAL.

Although the crash was not the specific fault of the airline, its President personally visited and apologized to the family of each crash victim. This completed, he resigned his office. He saw his duty beyond legal limits, beyond the mechanics of running the business, down to the interpersonal individual level of responsibility of delivering safe travel to his customers through his equipment and employees. In this he concluded that he had failed. This was to a degree the expected cultural response in Japan where legal exposures of claiming responsibility are considerably less. Never-the-less, it is a most fitting and empathetic response.

Quality Era business will need more leaders who see their duty from a similar perspective and are likewise personally committed to success by delivering quality products to their customers: Employees, including salespeople, will respect and follow such leadership, and customers will sense their confidence.

There will always be an unspoken communication between the producer of a product and the customer who uses it. This unspoken interaction should convey a message from the producer along the lines of "I made this better than you may at first recognize; as you use it you will understand that we took pains to make it correctly." The user's reaction should be that "I am finding this product increasingly pleasant in use. I appreciate its maker's concern for my satisfaction!" We each contribute to the world in which we live. The power of sales persuasion is the ability to elicit dreams of a better world through better products. The world already has too many shattered dreams. We must resolve to have those dreams *we sell* come true.

Summary

The implementation of a business strategy of differentiation through quality may well necessitate reviewing and modifying the existing motivational structures within the business. The determination of a business mission statement, including overall strategy, must often be developed in order to offer a clear direction for the design of processes and structures that must be brought to bear to address the challenges of the Quality Era. Only executive management is capable of establishing such a mission and strategy. Once these are established, processes and procedures must be visited and evaluated against the quality objectives. All such modification will challenge existing habits and attitudes, which must be altered to address the quality strategy. Thus the motivation of employees, including those in the sales group, must be enlisted for the quality strategy to succeed.

It is essential that there be leadership that can legitimately extend to each employee both tangible and intangible incentives. Employees must understand why the new initiatives will benefit them personally and why the changes in departmental functions are necessary. Managers must become closer to their employees. Salespeople must be prepared to appreciate a more team-oriented and broader set of functions. The benefits must be shared and enjoyed by all, and they will be both tangible and intangible – tangible because earnings and stability of the company mean security because the company can make and hold satisfied customers, and intangible because pride in company and joy in work can ensue. The vision of working with and for the best can motivate both managers and employees. To a remarkable degree, we each build the company and ultimately the world in which we must live.

References

[1] Neave, H. R., 1990. *The Deming Dimension*. Knoxville, TN: SPC Press, p. 388.

[2] Smith, Adam, 1759. *The Theory of Moral Sentiments*. Indianapolis: Liberty Fund, pp. 82–83.

[3] Macchiavelli, Niccolo. *The Prince*. New York: Bantam Books, p. 7.

[4] Deming, W. Edwards, 1986. *Out of the Crisis*. Cambridge, MA: MIT Press, p. 23.

[5] Yankelovich, Daniel and John Immerwahr, "Putting the Work Ethic to Work," *MIT Alumni Association Technology Review*, Vol. 86, November 1983.

Notes

1. Deming: We must adopt the new philosophy.

2. Contrast this attitude with that of Matsushita in Japan, whose employees submitted over six million suggestions for quality improvement in 1985.

3. Deming tells the story of receiving a phone call from a busy corporate executive who wanted to hire him for a day to "come over to our place and do for us what you did for the Japanese."

4. Deming: drive out fear (point #8).

5. I recall an incident from my days as an IBM sales manager when one of my salespeople went on a one-week vacation. A customer called our office expressing an interest in a computer system. I made a sales call with another member of the sales team and over the course of two days and three meetings we obtained an order equal to the entire year's sales quota for the salesperson on vacation, who had had a rather dismal performance so far that year. Some members of the sales unit suggested that he should take another vacation!

6. Deming point #6: institute on-the-job training.

7. Deming point #9: break down barriers between departments.

Conclusion

Selling is as old as the marketplace, and the marketplace is as old as mankind. The marketplace was made possible by language, which allowed negotiation, and by empathy, which added intuitive creativity and civility to the mix. People have always wanted to better their circumstances and have listened to those who have appeared capable of telling them how to do it. The merchant or peddler of yesterday, the marketing representative of today – they are all salespeople addressing the needs of customers. The new global market, with its amazing affluence of goods and services, is extremely recent. The global market – a major turning point in human history – is unfolding before this very generation.

A variety of competitive strategies will be taken by vendors within the global market. Differentiation through product quality is one of them. To this strategy must be added effective methodology for explaining the enhanced product value based on quality to customers. That is the job of Quality Era salespeople.

The new global market and the Quality Era call for broader, new approaches to selling and new structures for communicating value based on quality to customers, and for transmitting customers' attitudes and desires for value back into vendor organizations. Old attitudes of rigid departmental responsibility and narrow mission must give way, for they are destructive to Quality Era strategy. A company-wide, shared vision of quality in the form of comprehensive service to customers forms a powerful yet flexible foundation for facing the pressures of competition that will challenge all modern business. Quality strategy is not necessarily an inexpensive strategy. Indeed, should a business fail in attempting to adopt a pervasive quality strategy, it can be very costly. The adoption of a quality strategy must be taken as a most serious decision of strategic consequence. Once adopted, there can be no turning back.

Conclusion

Sales can play an important role in quality strategy. Sales-people frequently routinely develop an empathetic under-standing of customer attitudes and needs. As this knowledge is recognized and channeled effectively within the vendor organi-zation, many benefits can result. In the area of selling itself, management must adopt a process view of the sales continuum and surround it with structured support that yields consistency and quality in communication and service to customers. It is the well-drilled team following quality-capable processes that will win the consistent loyalty of customers, rather than the occa-sional lucky selling events that result by chance.

Management must structure the business so that, in effect, everyone sells by maintaining a focus on the ultimate objective of quality – the customer. People will continue to enjoy dealing with people, and the company that succeeds in making the customer feel valued regardless of whom he or she contacts is one step ahead in becoming a selling organization.

The greatest challenges of quality strategy implementation lie in the areas of employee motivation and commitment. Only as management intensely peruses the quality vision will creativ-ity and honesty in process innovation be enabled. Only as all employees feel they will share tangibly in the benefits of a quality strategy will they commit to, and focus on, its execution. The quality battle will be won or lost in the little, day-to-day issues of job performance, in the extra care that each individual is motivated to exert multiplied over the total number of employ-ees and over the total number of minutes, hours, days, and years. The empowerment and initiative that must be allowed each worker in this new economy means that management will be unable to monitor and check each action. Each employee must therefore supervise himself or herself. Without commitment to quality this freedom becomes license; with it a business can be transformed.

A vital link can be lost as businesses expand and departmen-talize. This is the direct and steady communication between the producer of an item and the customer. When the individual who produced an item was also the one who sold it and faced the customer, there was no gap. But such a gulf often exists today, and the company that focuses on quality in production must stay in synchrony with customer wishes or risk major loss. The sales function must be relinked with the design and production function for the improvement of both and for the benefit of the customer.

The businesses of the Quality Era should challenge salespeople and offer them new avenues for personal satisfaction. Motivation must be based on a broader pursuit of excellence along with monetary rewards.

Selling, or the interpersonal determination of need and the discussion of value, will always be a factor for some products and some companies. As the world moves toward more partnerships between manufacturer and distributor and between distributor and customer, personal professional salespeople will perform the introductions and negotiate the agreements. In the Quality Era professional selling will persist as the *responsible* interaction of personal persuasive force with human imagination.

INDEX